B628/BZX628 Managing 1: Organisations and people

Module Activities

Group A

The Open University, Walton Hall, Milton Keynes, MK7 6AA

First published 2010. This edition 2012.

Edited, designed and typeset by The Open University

Cover image: Fotosearch

Printed in the United Kingdom by Hobbs the Printers Limited, Brunel Road, Totton, Hampshire SO40 3WX.

ISBN 978 1 7800 7318 7

4.1

Contents

Week 1 What do managers do?	5
Week 2 Communicating and managing communication	13
Week 3 Problem-solving and decision-making	23
Week 4 Planning and control: making things happen	31
Week 5 Managing information	50
Week 6 TMA 01 preparation	57
Week 7 Understanding people at work	58
Week 8 Understanding leadership	68
Week 9 Working in groups and teams	76
Week 10 Recruiting and selecting staff (1)	84
Week 11 Recruiting and selecting staff (2)	102
Week 12 Managing performance (1)	116
Week 13 Managing performance (2)	124
Week 14 Learning and development at work	132
Week 15 TMA 02 preparation	142
Week 16 Organisational culture	143
Week 17 The organisation and the external environment	154
Week 18 Managing change (1)	163
Week 19 Managing change (2)	170
Weeks 20–22 EMA preparation	179
References	180

Week 1 What do managers do?

Introduction

Welcome to the first week of your studies. You probably have a variety of reasons for wanting to learn about management. The main one is almost certainly that you want to improve your effectiveness as a manager. If so, it helps to have a clear idea of what managers do and what is meant by managerial 'effectiveness'. To do this, you need to be able to identify your roles as a manager and those factors which influence your effectiveness – and these lie not only within yourself but also in your working environment. They include your job, your organisation, and the people you work with. Then you will need to diagnose what you might do to improve your own managerial performance, and take a first step to improve it.

We provide a number of views on the nature of management and what managers actually do. Then we look at the kinds of problems and issues that you deal with in your management role: we hope you will see that they have a common thread, whatever your particular sector of work. We offer you a variety of ways of looking at your job to help you to view your work more systematically and analytically. We consider some of the factors that can influence your effectiveness as a manager. Finally, we look at some of the problems that can arise when you move into management and how you might deal with them.

Week 1 Activities

- Activity 1 Introduce yourself to your tutor group and respond to at least one other student. (Allow 30 minutes for this activity.)
- Activity 2 Identify the key managerial roles you perform in your job. (Allow 20 minutes for this activity.)
- Activity 3 Post the results of Activity 2 to the Week 1 activity forum and read the contributions of other students. Compare managerial roles across several organisations and record similarities and differences in a message to the forum. (Allow 30 minutes for this activity.)
- Activity 4 Identify the main demands and constraints that restrict your choices about what, when and how you work. (Allow 20 minutes for this activity.)
- Activity 5 Identify one major pressure or stress over which you have influence and plan a remedial action. (Allow 20 minutes for this activity.)

Week 1 Readings

All readings are in *Managing and managing people*, Chapter 1 'What do managers do?'.

- Reading 1 What do managers actually do?
- Reading 2 Your job
- Reading 3 The demands, constraints and choices of your job
- Reading 4 Your management skills
- Reading 5 Transition into management
- Reading 6 Recognising pressure and avoiding stress
- Reading 7 Managing your time

Activity 1

Allow 30 minutes for this activity.

No two organisations are the same. No two management jobs are identical. No two situations are ever precisely the same. This explains why there is no one 'best way' of managing. What is appropriate in one organisation, at one time, in one situation and for one manager may not be appropriate in another. One of the benefits of studying management with other managers is that you can compare your situations. Understanding how your organisation, situation and practices are different from those of your fellow students provides you with valuable insights and learning that few textbooks can provide.

We, the module team, want to ensure that you make the most of this resource. So your first task of the module is to introduce yourself to your fellow students in your tutor group. The purpose of this activity is to 'meet' those you will be working with and get to know them a little.

It is quite usual to be a little nervous about this (and perhaps about beginning a course of study), but be reassured that other students will be feeling just as nervous!

Put up a message in the Tutor Group Forum (TGF) that includes:

- your name (or the name by which you prefer to be called)
- what your job is
- the sector you work in
- a little about your job
- an interesting fact about yourself (just one!).

(You don't have to give the name of the organisation you work for if you prefer not to. However, almost all students do so.) You will use this message to introduce yourself to your tutor and to your tutor group. Read the messages from your fellow students and respond to at least one of them.

Activity 1 outputs

- *A contribution to the TGF introducing yourself.*
- *A response to at least one other student.*

Readings 1 and 2

Do you sometimes feel that your management job is hard to describe? These first two readings should provide you with some of the reasons why this might be. Many managers find it is something of a relief to discover that they are not alone in struggling to make sense of what we call management. As you read *What do managers actually do?* in Chapter 1 of *Managing and managing people* consider the following questions:

1. Do you feel that you are responding to demands instead of being in control?
2. Do you follow any of Drucker's eight practices of effective managers?
3. How much do you think your effectiveness depends on you, your role, the people you work with and your organisation?
4. How important is each of these four elements in the effectiveness equation?

When you read with questions in mind about you and your own organisation, it helps you to process the meaning of what you are reading. Reading becomes active rather than passive, and helps you to remember what you have read.

Reading 2, *Your job*, in Chapter 1 explores in a different way what managers do. It considers managerial tasks and roles. As you read, consider the main day-to-day tasks in which you are engaged. Then take note of how Mintzberg categorises managerial activities into roles. Which roles are dominant in your job, or do you perform them equally? Are there any roles that you don't perform? Make notes as you read. These will help you with Activity 2.

Activity 2

Allow 20 minutes for this activity.

In this activity you will identify the Mintzberg roles you have performed in the last week.

- First, consider Mintzberg's 10 roles (which he places under three headings or categories). Then, think about the main managerial tasks you carried out last week.
- Identify THREE different tasks that occupied you most and match them to three of Mintzberg's 10 roles. Record the activity against the appropriate category in Table 1.1. The table will help you to structure your response to the activity. Next, think about any of Mintzberg's roles that you don't perform.
- Finally, with reference to Mintzberg's 10 roles, note what changes you would like to make in your roles to increase your contribution to the success of your organisation, or your part of the organisation. When

considering changes it is always good practice to identify who might be affected by the changes, a timescale and whether consultation with other people is needed. Record your responses in Table 1.1.

The purpose of this activity is to help you to be more aware of the management roles you perform in your job and to consider changes or improvements.

Table 1.1 Management roles

Mintzberg role	Brief description of the activity that matches the Mintzberg category
1	
2	
3	
Mintzberg roles I don't carry out	List:
Changes I could make in relation to Mintzberg's roles	List:
Who else would be affected by these changes	List:
The timescale of the potential changes	
Who I should consult	

It would be unusual if you carried out every one of Mintzberg's 10 roles, either in one week of work or in your management job overall. But it would also be unusual if you did not undertake several of the roles. The type and range depend on the context in which you work. It would also be unusual for all your managerial activities to have equal importance in your job. The learning point to be gained is that while many people are engaged in something called management, they are not engaged in exactly the same thing, as you will see when you compare your results with those of other students. The important difference is context. This determines your management roles in any given situation, including what type of organisation you work for.

Activity 2 output

- *A completed version of Table 1.1.*

Activity 3

Allow 30 minutes for this activity.

When you have completed Table 1.1, copy and paste it into a message to the Week 1 activity forum. As you read other students' contributions, compare them with your own. Then post a short message setting out your findings on the similarities and differences in your own management roles and those of other students. The purpose of this activity is for you to gain an understanding of the range of management roles adopted over a variety of management jobs, organisations and sectors.

Activity 3 outputs

- *A contribution to the Week 1 activity forum containing a completed copy of Table 1.1.*
- *A contribution to the Week 1 activity forum setting out your findings regarding the similarities or differences between your own management roles and those of other students.*

Reading 3

Reading 3, *The demands, constraints and choices of your job*, in Chapter 1 takes you more deeply into the context of management – the particular situation that you work in. The text sets out different types of demands on you – things you must do; different types of constraints – factors that limit what you can do; and choices that you may have. As you read, consider your job in terms of each type of demand, constraint and choice. This will prepare you for Activity 4.

Activity 4

Allow 20 minutes for this activity.

Consider the demands made on you when you carry out your job. Rate each type of demand from 1 (low) to 10 (high), and provide an example in cases where a demand is high. Record your scores in Table 1.2. Then consider the factors that place constraints on what you can do. Rate these in the same way and record them. Provide an example in cases where a constraint is high.

Table 1.2 Demands and constraints

Demands	Rating	Example	Constraints	Rating	Example
Manager-imposed			Resource limitations		
Peer-imposed			Legal regulations		
Externally-imposed			Union agreements		
System-imposed			Technological limitations		
Staff-imposed			Physical location		
Self-imposed			Policies and procedures		
			Attitudes and expectations		
			Ethical considerations		
			Environmental concerns		

(Source: based on Stewart, 1982)

Activity 4 should provide you with a picture of the demands and constraints you are subject to. The choices you have in your job will be greater when you have few demands and few constraints, although not many managers find themselves in that position. Most managers face substantial demands, but often from only two or three sources. Similarly, most managers have a number of constraints but not in all the areas shown. Activity 4 demonstrates how your context shapes what, how and when your work, and that of your work group, is done. It also has an important purpose in this module too. When you are resolving workplace issues you will always need to consider demands, constraints and choices. You will also need to consider the extent to which you have an influence over some demands and constraints. As you carried out Activity 4, you may have begun thinking about this!

Activity 4 output

- *A completed version of Table 1.2.*

Readings 4, 5, 6 and 7

These readings all deal with pressure on managers and the stress that can result from too much pressure. If you have been trained in managing pressure, stress and time, it is appropriate for you to skim read here. Skim reading is explained in *The Manager's Good Study Guide* on p. 34.

Reading 4, *Your management skills*, in Chapter 1 sets out some recognised skills that managers need in order to be effective. Note that if your capabilities don't match what your job requires, then the result is likely to be frustration and stress. However, the reason you are studying this module is likely to be to improve your skills and capabilities. In this case, you are taking active steps to remedy this situation. Reading 5, *Transition into management*, in Chapter 1 deals with a particular situation: that of the new manager moving from 'operating' to managing. Any transition has the potential to cause stress. However, the understanding that the transition is a process and that there are actions a person can take to become an effective manager is likely to be stress-reducing. You may have already experienced this particular transition. If you are experiencing it now, however, or made the transition some time ago but not entirely successfully, consider what kinds of adjustments you could make.

Reading 6, *Recognising pressure and avoiding stress*, in Chapter 1 considers common causes of stress with the emphasis on management and managers. This reading will be useful however long you have been a manager. What particular pressures are you under this week? What methods of reducing stress are open to you? Reading 7, *Managing your time*, in Chapter 1 takes you through the main points of time management. As you read, make a note of the ways in which your time is used and what you might do to save time. The notes you make while you are reading will help you to carry out Activity 5.

Activity 5

Allow 20 minutes for this activity.

This activity is designed to identify one main pressure or stress in your work as a manager and what you could do about it. Consider all the sources of pressure and stress covered in Readings 4 to 7. Identify just one that currently affects you most, and one action that you can take to reduce it. Say how you could carry out this action. When you are deciding on what action you will take, remember the demands and constraints that will restrict the choices you have. If you find that you have identified a pressure or stress about which you can do nothing, or not easily, then select one that you have more influence or control over. You might discuss with your line manager the major pressure you can do nothing about. Use Table 1.3 for the activity.

Table 1.3 Stresses and actions

The major stress factor in my work:
What I will do about it:
How I will do this:

It is likely that your responses to the activity focussed on the last two readings, and possibly the last one of all. The kinds of pressures set out in Reading 6, *Recognising pressure and avoiding stress*, are easier to recognise than to deal with. Time management issues, covered in Reading 7, *Managing your time*, are often easier to deal with.

If you were now to review your first week's activities you would see that you have created a profile of your job:

- the roles you perform
- the demands of the job and the constraints that limit your choices over how you carry out your task, when and how
- one important aspect of your job that creates most pressure or stress.

At the same time, you have planned an action that you can carry out to improve your effectiveness. You have begun networking with your fellow students and had the opportunity to gain insight into organisations other than the one you work for.

Activity 5 output

- *A completed version of Table 1.3.*

Week 1 activity outputs

- A contribution to the TGF introducing yourself.
- A response to at least one other student's introductory message.
- A completed version of Table 1.1.
- A contribution to Week 1 activity forum containing a completed copy of Table 1.1.
- A contribution to Week 1 activity forum setting out your findings on the similarities/differences between your management roles and those of other students.
- A completed version of Table 1.2.
- A completed version of Table 1.3.

Learning outcomes

After completing this set of activities and readings you should be able to:

- understand what is meant by management and managerial effectiveness
- identify the roles which you are fulfilling in your work as a manager
- identify managerial activities that contribute to managerial effectiveness
- identify a cause of stress in your managerial life from a range covering mismatches between capabilities and role, player–manager tension and everyday stressors
- understand time pressures and the need for time management
- plan one action to reduce stress.

Activity three still to be completed.

Week 2 Communicating and managing communication

Introduction

Communication is a core management skill. But what does it mean to communicate effectively and is there one best way that will work in every situation? What skills do we need? How can we communicate about technical matters while at the same time helping our people to feel valued and motivated? Communication skills and knowledge vary considerably between individuals, as do communication problems in different organisations. For this reason, in presenting the topic of communication, we have covered a range of sub-topics from interpersonal skills to the use of new technology.

When people are asked about what is done well and less well in their organisation, the most frequent criticism is about communications. They often criticise the quality of senior managers' communications with those at lower levels of the organisation. But communication *can* be managed well and the materials here should help you to achieve this.

This study session is important for a different reason too. This week you are presented with a first problem-solving activity. You will identify a situation in which you would like to improve communication and work out what you need to do to make the improvement.

Week 2 Activities

- Activity 1 Assess the communication climate in your immediate work environment using an inventory. (Allow 1 hour for this activity, longer if you involve others.)
- Activity 2 Analyse a request you have made to a more junior person and suggest improvements. (Allow 30 minutes for this activity.)
- Activity 3 Identify a workplace communication issue in which you are involved and suggest how it might be resolved. (Allow 2 hours for this activity.)

Week 2 Readings

All readings are in *Managing and managing people*, Chapter 2 'Communicating and managing communication'.

- Reading 1 The communication climate
- Reading 2 Theories of communication

- Reading 3 Understanding communication
- Reading 4 Barriers to communication
- Reading 5 Beyond the words: paralanguage and non-verbal communication
- Reading 6 Communication skills
- Reading 7 Communication and new technology (optional)
- Reading 8 What are meetings for? (optional)
- Reading 9 Making meetings more effective (optional)

Reading 1

How would you describe how your own organisation 'feels'? Do people talk to each other in an open and friendly way, or is it a place where people don't like to admit to mistakes? This first reading, *The communication climate*, in Chapter 2 sets out key features of communication in organisations and their impact. Note that the communication climate includes all information needs and how they are met as well as the way in which people communicate about tasks and provide feedback on performance. As you read it may help to make notes of the key points and how communication 'works' in your work group. The reading is directly relevant to the first activity, which follows.

Activity 1

Allow 1 hour for this activity (longer if you involve others).

In this activity you will sample your organisation's communication climate, using an inventory. Measuring the communication climate of an entire organisation is difficult, but a communication climate can exist between as few as two people. You can therefore use it with the people you supervise, or you can complete it yourself with your line manager in mind. In this case, the 'supervisor' referred to in the inventory will be your boss. The purpose of the activity is for you to be able to assess systematically your 'local' communication climate and identify any areas to work on in a later activity.

Before you involve other people in this activity, you will need to think about whether you will share some or all of the results with them.

Download the inventory from Module Resources on the module website and follow the instructions for completing and working out the scores. Your tutor will provide additional guidance if you need it. Respond to each question as honestly as possible. Record your inventory score and briefly describe the communication climate using Table 2.1.

Table 2.1 Communication climate inventory

Total 'defensive score'	Score:
Total 'supportive score'	Score:
The main negative aspects of communication with my boss/in my work group	List:
The main positive aspects of communication with my boss/in my work group	List:
My thoughts in 50 words	

When you calculated the final scores, did you find that they matched your initial feelings about the communication climate in your work group or with your boss? You may have thought the communication climate was unremarkable or average, only to find it was better than you expected. Alternatively, you might have thought it was relatively good only to see that it was worse than expected. This is often what people find when they consider specific aspects of a situation they have thought about only in general terms before.

While completing the inventory – or if you asked members of your work group to complete it – you may have had or collected some views on how the communication climate could be improved. You will have the opportunity to consider these later.

Activity 1 output

- *A completed version of Table 2.1.*

Readings 2 and 3

Reading 2, *Theories of communication*, in Chapter 2 provides background. A key concept here is empathy, and this is clearly defined. The reading underlines why empathy is fundamental to effective communication. As you will see, empathy does not mean agreeing with another person, but being able to place yourself in their situation in order to understand better the other person's perceptions or feelings. Reading 3, *Understanding communication*, in Chapter 2 sets out ways in which we 'read' the intentions of speakers, interpret meaning, understand the language of power and status, and see how conversation is controlled by speakers. These two readings, which are more theoretical than the others on communication, are designed to increase your understanding and awareness when you are communicating.

Activity 2

Allow 30 minutes for this activity.

This activity is designed to build awareness of how you communicate by assessing a request you have made in writing to a more junior person. The request may have been made in memo form or by email. We would prefer a written message so that you can see exactly the words that you used. If your requests are generally made verbally, recall what you said as accurately as possible.

The request should be more substantial than, for example, 'would it be convenient to move our Thursday meeting from 10.00 to 14.00?' but about 250 words long.

Identify three main features of the language used and record them in the pro forma provided below (Table 2.2). The main features are likely to be the degree of empathy used and 'politeness' factors, dependent on issues such as social distance, relative power and degree of imposition. Then say how the request might have been improved. The locution (what you said) and the illocution (what you intended) will be clear to you. However, if you had feedback on the perlocution – how your request was received and interpreted – then use this feedback to inform your suggested improvement.

Table 2.2 Features of a request to a direct report/more junior person

Who the request was made to, and their status; that is, their level in the hierarchy relative to your position:
The wording of the request:
Three key features of the language used in the message: 1. 2. 3.
How I would improve the message:

This activity should have helped you to gain insight into the language you use, even if you couldn't see many ways of improving the request you made. One way of improving the wording of a request is to take the one you wrote to a more junior person and redraft it to a more senior person, then analyse the differences.

Activity 2 output

- *A completed version of Table 2.2.*

Activity 3 Part 1

Identify a current situation in which you would like to improve communication. The situation must be one over which you have control or influence, involving a small number of people, for example, your work group, you and a member of your work group or you and your line manager. The situation may be a general one, for example, where communication always seems somewhat unsatisfactory – perhaps a 'climate' issue – or a specific one, for example, communication in a team in which some or all members are not 'co-located', that is, working in the same geographical place. For the moment, just make a note of the situation. You will return to it after some more reading. Note that we are continuing to look at the interpersonal issues in communication, so the situation you identify should concern one of these.

Readings 4–6

Readings 4, 5 and 6 are essential and you should read them regardless of the situation you identified in Activity 2. All the readings are relevant to managing and there may be content that will help you to explore the communication situation you have identified and, importantly, decide on the actions you need to take. It would be useful to take notes as you read: these can take the form of key points.

Reading 4, *Barriers to communication*, in Chapter 2 covers basic ways in which communication can be made more difficult. This reading should allow you to identify specific barriers and how barriers can be reduced or removed, particularly if you identified a 'general' need to improve communication.

Reading 5, *Beyond the words: paralanguage and non-verbal communication*, in Chapter 2 covers behaviours we use when communicating. These not only help to convey and support the meaning of what is said, but we gauge these behaviours in others to assess how they are feeling, whether they are trustworthy and what their intentions are.

Reading 6, *Communication skills*, in Chapter 2 covers two vital communication skills for the manager: listening and questioning, and what types to use in particular situations. Activity 2 provided an opportunity to gain deeper understanding of a message; be confident in building on this to assess your listening and questioning skills (as well as considering the skills of others involved in the situation you identified).

Readings 7–9

Depending on the communication situation you chose in Activity 3 Part 1, you have some choice regarding which texts you read now. Reading 7 is important if you use new technology for communication and the situation you identified involves communication which is not, or not always, face to face. Readings 8 and 9 are important if the situation you identified concerns participating in or running meetings. You should skim read those you don't intend to cover in any depth. Again, it would be useful to take notes as you read.

Reading 7, *Communication and new technology*, in Chapter 2 deals with different media and their relative capacity to carry the 'richness' of communication that we associate with face-to-face conversation. While it may seem sensible to use the technology that is most 'fit for purpose', this is often not what happens in organisations. The reading is interesting even if the communication situation does not involve new technology: the case study could illustrate the typical office of tomorrow as organisations try to reduce their costs and their carbon footprints.

Readings 8 and 9, both in Chapter 2, cover meetings. Reading 8, *What are meetings for*, deals with types of meetings. Reading 9, *Making meetings more effective*, will be useful if you plan and organise meetings. If the communication situation you identified concerns meetings, you may realise that you are trying to cover too much in a meeting and that this is a source of difficulty. In this case, you might want to read Reading 7 to see what might be achieved in other ways using new technology.

If the issue you identified concerns written communication or giving presentations, you will find relevant material in *The Manager's Good Study Guide* (see pp. 37–59 and pp. 99–102).

Activity 3 Part 2

Allow 2 hours for this activity.

This activity takes the important step beyond analysis to action. Its purpose is to encourage you to consider and set out what you will do about a problem or how you will improve a situation. There is a standard model for problem-solving, and you will learn more about it next week. At this stage, the headings of this model are sufficient. These are:

- Problem identification and description
- Analysis
- Conclusions to the analysis
- Recommendations
- Advantages, disadvantages and implications.

Problem identification and description: In Activity 3 Part 1 you identified a situation in which you feel communication could or should be improved, and which is under your control or influence. Now you have completed some more reading, you should be able to identify and describe this situation in a more precise way. Set out to whom the situation is a problem and why. Write this in the appropriate section of the response table provided (Table 2.3). An example of a completed table (Table 2.4) is also provided to guide you on the amount and type of detail necessary for this module. If you were to write a report on the issue for your line manager or someone more senior (or your organisation) you might include more, or less, detail and you might have to explain (or avoid!) some of the more technical terms you are learning on this module.

Analysis: What is going on in this situation? Consider the communication climate. Consider the main barriers to communication. Consider the behaviour of each party in the communication situation – how they initiate dialogue, how they respond to others, how they shape or control conversation, whether they use inappropriate paralanguage and body language. Consider your own skills and whether these might be contributory factors. Consider the context and whether the medium of communication is appropriate. If the situation involves formal meetings, consider whether there are issues involving the organisation of meetings or roles. When you have worked out what you think is 'going on' in the situation, write this in the appropriate place in Table 2.3.

Conclusions to the analysis: Here you need to draw together the main points of your analysis into one or more concluding statements. Look at Table 2.4 for an example.

Recommendations: These can be set out as a list or as an action plan which covers what you will do to improve the situation. Use a simple design of action plan that you use at work. All recommendations should be SMART – that is, Specific (they must state clearly what is to be achieved); Measurable (they must state how you will know whether you have achieved your aim); Agreed (they must be agreed with anyone who will be affected, although this may or may not be necessary in this case); Realistic (they must be achievable within the constraints of the situation, such as the time and money available, and relate one to another); and Timed (a target time needs to be set). Often, in everyday problem-solving, we don't specify 'SMART' recommendations because much is obvious. We are likely to ask ourselves: What exactly do I want to achieve? Given that I can't do all that I would like, what's the most important thing I should/could do? How much time have I to spend on this? What kind of timeframe is needed? How will I know whether the plan has worked? These sorts of considerations should be evident in the recommendations.

Advantages, disadvantages and implications: No plan is ever ideal. Set out the advantages and disadvantages – the strengths and weaknesses – of your action plan. Review your plan if the costs are greater than the benefits. If the advantages do not outweigh thc disadvantages, you may need to amend your plan. Invariably, a course of action has implications. For example, in the case of a solution involving new technology there may be a need to buy equipment and to train staff.

Table 2.3 Communication improvement

Problem identification and description:
Analysis:
Conclusions to the analysis:
Recommendations:
Advantages, disadvantages and implications:

Table 2.4 below is an example of a response. Not all the ideas and information that the writer considered are included, only those that seemed most relevant and important and which addressed the problem. Whenever you identify, analyse and suggest ways to solve a problem, you are likely to record only a small proportion of your thinking. This would be the case if you wrote a report at work: you would aim to be concise and focussed on key issues. The example provided concerns a relatively small problem which can be quite easily resolved. Your own may be similar, or more complex and difficult to resolve or improve. Whatever communication situation you have chosen, you should make sure that you are in a position to control or influence the situation, and that there aren't important, far-reaching implications beyond your control. Thus, you will need to consider and separate out your communication problem into components: you may not be able to deal with all aspects of it, but just those over which you have sufficient influence to take action.

Table 2.4 An example of a completed response table

Communication improvement: an example	
Problem identification and description:	The monthly project team meetings I organise are relatively unproductive. The decisions made (by consensus) are sometimes poor and one team member has a negative attitude. Conflicts often arise from this. The situation is a problem because it affects the morale of the team and the poor decision-making affects various aspects of the project.
Analysis:	Possible reasons for situation: 1 The agendas are long and there's a lot of information to deliver, not all of which requires discussion. 2 There's insufficient time to discuss important issues. Decisions are often reviewed at the next month's meeting because people have second thoughts. 3 Jan's presence is disruptive; it's usual for her to disagree with everyone else's ideas, while having few suggestions of her own. When I spoke to her after the last meeting about being constructive in her criticisms she said she instantly sees the problem but not the solution. 4 I'm not very good at managing Jan, i.e. dealing with that kind of conflict.
Conclusions to the analysis:	The problem appears to be caused by insufficient attention to the agenda to see (a) what information can be delivered in advance and (b) what needs discussing. This leaves too little time for adequate discussion, which is why decisions are revisited. My own skills in handling conflict (i.e. Jan) are a factor.
Recommendations	1 Attend to the agenda next week. Remove all information-only items and ask for short, written reports that can be circulated by email two weeks in advance of the meeting. Provide deadline for written reports. 2 Identify the items that require most consideration. Circulate a description of each one or two weeks before each meeting to allow 'thinking time'. Invite initial suggestions via email. (Electronic group messaging would be good for this; it's easy for a person to be left off an email circulation list.) Ask team members to come to meetings with at least one suggestion in mind. 3 Acknowledge Jan's ability to 'see the problems' in possible solutions but involve her and others in seeing if 'the problem' can be resolved, worked around, etc. That is, try to turn a negative into a positive. 4 Agree the changes with team members as soon as new agenda is completed next week. 5 Review how the new system is working after two meetings.

Communication improvement: an example	
Advantages, disadvantages and implications:	**Advantages:** 1 The time saved by circulating information in advance will provide additional time for discussion. 2 Advance circulation of important discussion items should allow team members, and especially Jan, to come to the meeting with suggestions.
	Disadvantages: 1 The plan may not work if people don't make the time to consider the discussion items and come to the meeting with suggestions; some important pieces of information may not be given the attention they need. 2 Jan may still not come up with suggestions; lack of time at meetings may be an excuse. If she continues to be disruptive, I'll need to think of something else. 3 Looking at Jan's emphasis on problems could lead to new negative responses from her.
	Implications: 1 The administrative tasks will change; the work in organising the meeting will be spread over a longer timescale and Jenny, the secretary, will need to 'chase' information-only items. 2 If the new system works well, we may have to buy group conferencing software which will have resource and training implications.

Working on your first problem-based activity of the module was probably not easy. However, you should have an action plan to discuss and put into place at work straight away. In general, the better your analysis, your solution and your scrutiny of the possible weaknesses and implications, the better you should be able to resolve issues and improve situations in such a way that they are not likely to recur. Working on this activity you probably had to work hard to keep your focus on the specific issue. You may have realised that there are a number of issues related to the one you identified. We look in more detail at this interrelatedness in the next session; few problems are isolated ones. That's why managing is messy rather than technical and mechanistic.

Activity 3 Parts 1 and 2 output

- *A completed version of Table 2.3.*

Week 2 activity outputs

1 A completed version of Table 2.1.

2 A completed version of Table 2.2.

3 A completed version of Table 2.3.

Learning outcomes

After completing this set of activities and readings you should be able to:

- Understand the importance of effective communication
- Understand the process of communication
- Identify barriers to communication and help to lower them where you have control or influence
- Communicate more effectively
- Improve communication in situations in which communication is poor and over which you have control or influence.

Week 3 Problem-solving and decision-making

Introduction

This week we introduce you to another core management skill: problem-solving. Today's employers need managers with a capacity for problem-solving – and the kind of flexibility of thinking associated with it. At times organisations must deal with fast-changing situations which need rapid and effective action. This is the kind of problem-solving we hear about in the business news. More often, however, managers are continually solving problems in their day-to-day management. There are things to be put right because something has gone wrong, expectations have changed, something needs improvement, or something new needs to be introduced. Problem-solving, then, isn't just about 'problems' in a negative sense. Investigating a situation, working out options and deciding on the 'best' solution for the context in which you are working help your organisation to stay on course to meet its objectives. Problem-solving helps an organisation improve how it goes about its work, making the most of the available resources and using them more effectively and efficiently.

Some organisations – for example, those who are committed to continuous improvement – often want managers to 'find' problems. That is, they want managers to look actively for ways of doing things better as part of an organisation-wide 'quality culture'. If you work in such an organisation, problem-finding and problem-solving – and making improvements – may be a routine part of your work.

Week 3 Activities

- Activity 1 Identify the types of problems you encounter at work. (Allow 30 minutes for this activity.)
- Activity 2 Identify a recent (resolved) management problem you have dealt with or were involved in and the steps taken to resolve it. (Allow 45 minutes for this activity.)
- Activity 3 Compare the steps taken to solve the problem with those of a model of problem-solving and a framework for decision-making. Identify three strengths and three weaknesses in the approach taken in dealing with your workplace problem. (Allow 45 minutes for this activity.)
- Activity 4 Post the results of Activities 2 and 3 to the Week 3 activity forum and read the contributions of other students. Draw out and record three key learning points from these contributions about the different ways in which managers in other organisations currently go about problem-solving. (Allow 1 hour for this activity.)

Week 3 Readings

All readings are in *Managing and managing people*, Chapter 3 'Problem-solving and decision-making'.

- Reading 1 Solving problems and making decisions in organisations
- Reading 2 Problem-solving – a framework
- Reading 3 Making decisions: comparing options and making choices
- Reading 4 The problem with problem-solving and decision-making
- Reading 5 Problem-solving in action: an example

Reading 1

Why, when faced with a situation, do we sometimes know instantly what to do and at other times struggle to understand what is happening? Why do our solutions to problems sometimes not work and sometimes work very well? The answers to these questions lie in, first, the nature of the problem and second, our understanding of what problem-solving involves (and when to do it). Reading 1, *Solving problems and making decisions in organisations*, in Chapter 3 sets out the difference between decision-making and problem-solving. Note that it is not always necessary to solve a problem. The same problem may recur routinely and require the same solution each time, so all that is required is the decision to implement the same solution. Situations of this kind happen daily in organisations: a person tells us they will leave to work for another employer and a new person needs to be recruited. Unless the job of the person leaving needs redesigning for some reason, there is no 'problem' to address. At other times, there will be an issue to address. As you read, consider the issues you have addressed at work recently that required you to solve a problem. Make notes as you read to help you with Activity 1, in which you will describe a recent work problem that you needed to resolve.

Activity 1

Allow 30 minutes for this activity.

What types of problems do you typically encounter at work? Are the solutions obvious and routine, or just the opposite? This activity is designed to help you recognise the kinds of problems you encounter at work along with the solutions you choose. Using the problem–solution matrix (Table 3.1) in Reading 1 consider the four different types of problems and solutions and how often or seldom each occurs in the course of your job. Record this information in Table 3.1 below. Then, identify two examples of each type of problem–solution that occurs and describe them briefly. You may be reluctant to consider that you might deal with unknown problems with known solutions. Or you may think that you never encounter unknown problems with unknown solutions, but consider all the cases in which a problem has not been evident but you decided to improve the effectiveness or efficiency of a system or service or a routine activity. This might have been part of a wider initiative to improve quality in general across the organisation.

Do not be concerned if you cannot complete the whole of Table 3.1 – you may not encounter a problem–solution type. However, you should be able to complete at least one section of the table for one problem–solution type, however small (or large) the problem/solutions of that type you deal with at work and however infrequently.

Table 3.1 My problem–solution types

Situations in which there is a known problem/unknown solution	
Frequency	Daily, weekly, less often, seldom or never
Example 1	
Example 2	
Situations in which there is a known problem/known solution	
Frequency	Daily, weekly, less often, seldom or never
Example 1	
Example 2	
Situations in which there is an unknown problem/unknown solution	
Frequency	Daily, weekly, less often, seldom or never
Example 1	
Example 2	
Situations in which there is an unknown problem/known solution	
Frequency	Daily, weekly, less often, seldom or never
Example 1	
Example 2	

(Source: based on Peckham, 1996)

While carrying out this activity, you may have realised how many routine problems you encounter that require routine solutions. It is often the case that we do not recognise them as problems or our decisions/actions as solutions: investigation will have been minimal. You may also have realised that at least some of these situations might have benefited from some analysis. Whatever your completed version of Table 3.1 contains, thinking about the types of problems and solutions will be useful preparation for Activity 2.

Activity 1 output

- *A completed version of Table 3.1.*

Activity 2

Allow 45 minutes for this activity.

For Activity 2 you need to identify a management problem that required your investigation and resolution which you resolved recently. It is important that you can recall the sequence of events, the people involved and what happened. We have provided questions in the output table, Table 3.2, as an aid to recalling what happened and to thinking about the events and the people involved. Your completed version of Table 3.2 should be about 150 words in length.

Consider the questions in Table 3.2 one by one. Often we recognise a problem by its symptoms (the ways in which it shows itself) and only then are we able to state 'what the problem is'. Problems also tend to 'belong' to someone: the problem-holder will often seek help by saying 'I have a problem with ...'. In a team situation, the team may own the problem, for example, 'We have a problem with ...'. Usually the problem will involve others. A problem involving a communication system will involve all the people in the system. It's likely that the problem is most serious for the last person in the chain of communication who is not receiving the information required, or not receiving it in the right form. If people are involved in the problem, or situation, often they will need to be involved in the solution, so it is always useful to identify them as soon as possible.

The remaining questions are straightforward: say why you think the problem arose, how much investigation you had to do to discover the reasons why the problem occurred, and what needed to be done, why and by whom. Then try to remember whether several solutions were possible. If so, how did you choose between them? Perhaps some of the 'solutions' that you might have chosen were not options at all. Perhaps you had some genuine choices. If so, how was the choice made? On what basis? After the solution was implemented did it 'work', that is, did it resolve the problem or address the situation in the way intended? Now consider the list of people you identified earlier as being involved in the problem. Were these people consulted at each stage? If not, when were they consulted (if at all)? Next, consider what influenced the way you went about solving your problem, including how you investigated it, the solutions open to you and how you made your choice. You may remember reading in Week 1 about the demands made on managers and the constraints that limit your choices of action. Demands and constraints can be difficult to identify. Often they are so familiar to us that we do not see them – we 'take them for granted'. For example, we may work in the kind of organisation in which it would be unacceptable to act without consultation; in another organisation we might be expected to consult only in particular circumstances. Such expectations shape our practices. Finally, note anything you consider to be important about the problem or solution that the list of questions doesn't cover.

Table 3.2 Describing my own problem

What was the problem and how did you recognise it?
To whom was it a problem (the 'problem-holder') and who else was involved?
What caused the problem?
How much investigation did you have to do to find out what caused the problem and how did you do this?
What needed to be done, why and by whom?
Were there several solutions to the problem? If so, how did you choose between them?
What was the outcome of the chosen solution?
Was there communication with those involved at every stage?
What demands and constraints influenced how you investigated the problem and chose a solution?
What other issues do you consider to be important?

We hope this activity has helped you to focus on some important issues in problem-solving, which we look at in more detail shortly. In completing this activity, you may well have had ideas about how you might have handled the problem differently. This is often the case when we take time to reflect on our actions or practices. It is an important part of the learning process when we try to improve our skills and effectiveness.

Activity 2 output

- *A completed version of Table 3.2.*

Readings 2 and 3

Readings 2 and 3 take you through a framework for problem-solving and for making decisions. Reading 2, *Problem-solving – a framework*, in Chapter 3 sets out the problem-solving process in a clear, linear fashion. However, as you will see later, the process is an iterative one: problem-solvers move forwards and backwards through it. Reading 3, *Making decisions: comparing options and making choices*, in Chapter 3 also sets out a framework. This looks simple, but using it can take a long time.

As you progress through Readings 2 and 3, bear in mind your response to Activity 2. This will prepare you for Activity 3, in which you will compare how you identified, investigated and resolved your work problem with the 'ideal' problem-solving and decision-making frameworks set out in the two readings.

Activity 3

Allow 45 minutes for this activity.

Activities that are designed to expose the difference between what we did and an 'ideal' can be difficult. Often we can feel quite defensive and try to justify our actions to show that there were no other ways. However, we need to be able to think about the possibility that we could have acted differently. Doing different things might have been more effective. It is an important way in which we learn: we see a conflict between what we know (what we did) and new information (what we might have done). We resolve this conflict by changing our thinking so that next time we act differently. This should improve our effectiveness. You may find this activity a little uncomfortable. Learning itself can be uncomfortable, as we look at long-held views and are required to question them.

Activity 3 asks you to consider your responses to Activity 2 and compare how you handled your problem with the problem-solving and decision-making frameworks set out in the two readings. First, remember that the frameworks are 'ideals'. Problem-solving is rarely simple and straightforward, and decision-making can be difficult for a number of reasons.

As you compare your responses to Activity 2 with these frameworks, make notes about the extent to which you used the main stages in the problem-solving framework to solve your problem. If you had more than one solution available, note to what extent you used steps in the decision-making framework. Note that the 'phases' of problem-solving and decision-making correspond to particular questions in Table 3.2. Questions 1–5 fall into the investigation phase, Question 6 into the solution phase, and Questions 7 and 8 into the implementation stage which is covered next week. When people make this comparison many find that the investigation stage – the analysis of the problem – is often overlooked.

Now, using the notes you have made, identify three strengths in the approach you took and three weaknesses. Record these strengths and weaknesses in Table 3.3.

Table 3.3 Strengths and weaknesses

Strength 1
Strength 2
Strength 3
Weakness 1
Weakness 2
Weakness 3

A typical set of strengths and weaknesses might be:

Strengths

- I took time to consult the key people involved. That meant that the solution was quite easy to implement – there was no opposition.
- I systematically looked at the options open to me. I considered how each could help to solve my problem.
- I set SMART objectives for the solution.

Weaknesses

- I didn't investigate the problem fully. Looking back, there was something that I needed to consider.
- I didn't think enough about the needs of the 'problem-holder' – me! I thought too much about others' needs and the solution was unsatisfactory.
- I need to think more about the implications of solutions: even solutions need investigation! I could not choose the best solution because it would have affected other parts of the organisation. My line manager said this would not be acceptable.

Note that a strength might also be linked to a weakness. The list above suggests that while there was a high level of consultation, too much account of the needs of others was taken. It also suggests that consultation did not lead to full investigation of the problem. Perhaps consultation did not focus much on this aspect of problem-solving. Note also that the potential outcomes of the possible solutions were carefully looked at. However, implications were not considered sufficiently. Often the strength is that we did think about something carefully and acted appropriately. Often a weakness is that we did not divide up our time well. This might be because we did not ask for help from experts or our managers.

Activity 3 output

- *A completed version of Table 3.3.*

Activity 4

Allow 1 hour for this activity.

You may now be interested in how other organisations solve their problems. Are the problems that managers face at your level in other organisations similar to yours? Do other managers solve problems in the same way that you do? How influenced are they by the demands and constraints that exist in their organisations? Activity 4 is an opportunity to find out.

This activity requires you to use the Week 3 activity forum to post your outputs from Activities 2 and 3 to your fellow students. Write a message to which you attach copies of the Activity 2 and 3 outputs, or in which you copy and paste the outputs. The latter method is preferable because it will be easier for other students to read your contributions. If you or your organisation would prefer not to reveal some issues in your problem then you will need to edit your output in some other way so that you do not mention the names of people, departments or organisations. You can use different names. (However, take care to keep a copy of your original output for your TMA.)

Read the contributions of other students and draw three key learning points from their inputs. You may be surprised to find that the postings show that the way problem-solving is approached is similar in a number of ways. Were you surprised to find that many problems focus on people management? This is often the case. Did you find it interesting that managers from different organisations and different sectors are subject to quite different demands and constraints, leading to different kinds of solution to similar problems?

When you have decided on your three key learning points, record them in a Word file. There is no template for this activity. Label the Word file 'Week 3 Activity 4'. During the module you will collect many activity output files that you will need for your assessed work. Take care to label the files systematically so that you can easily identify the ones you want when you need them.

Activity 4 outputs

- *Contribution to the Week 3 activity forum.*
- *Three key learning points.*

Readings 4 and 5

Reading 4, *The problem with problem-solving and decision-making*, in Chapter 3 connects the previous readings on formal frameworks for problem-solving with how problem-solving is done in the workplace. It discusses how complex and messy problem-solving is in practice. This probably makes problem-solving more recognisable in your organisation. We expect that when you solve work problems as you study, you will find that they are complex and messy. Often you will not be able to use 'ideal' solutions: you will find that you have to choose the one that best fits the present circumstances. In other words, solutions must fit the context in which you work and the circumstances of the moment. Reading 5, *Problem-solving in action: an example*, in Chapter 3 provides an example of problem-solving in action.

Take a moment to consider your conclusion about problem-solving. While the process of problem-solving appears to be straightforward and logical, there are many factors that prevent such a systematic journey from problem identification to solution and implementation. Problem-solving is iterative but it is an essential process. The best solutions will often not be possible. This is because of organisational factors, time and other resources, political agendas, swiftly-changing priorities and other factors like these. But problem-solving should allow you to arrive at a situation which, if not ideal, is an improvement.

Week 3 activity outputs

1 A completed version of Table 3.1.
2 A completed version of Table 3.2.
3 A completed version of Table 3.3.
4 Contribution to the Week 3 activity forum.
5 Three key learning points.

Learning outcomes

After completing this set of activities and readings you should be able to:

- understand the problem-solving process
- understand the decision-making process and how to decide between options
- identify the effectiveness of your approach to problem-solving and decision-making and understand the ways in which improvements can be made
- understand the organisational context in which problems are solved and why solutions are often less than ideal.

Week 4 Planning and control: making things happen

Introduction

Planning and controlling activities successfully is a vital management role. Whatever a manager's *particular* role, it is inevitable that planning and controlling activities will be central to it. Management control is a topic that most managers find highly relevant and immediately useful. This week we guide you step by step through the planning process and show you how to monitor and control activities.

The task of making things happen on time, on budget and as planned, of course, is a difficult one which will often require problem-solving. Your study last week prepared you for the task of problem-solving. This week we bring problem-solving and the new topic of management control together so that you can identify and set out a solution to a management control problem that you are currently experiencing, or have experienced recently. You will realise from your reading last week that by 'problem' we do not necessarily mean that something is 'wrong' and needs fixing. It could be that expectations have changed or improvements are desirable.

Be prepared for a challenging week, but one from which you can reap rich rewards in terms of your effectiveness as a manager.

Week 4 Activities

- Activity 1 Analyse a micro operation that you manage in terms of inputs, outputs and processes. (Allow 20 minutes for this activity.)
- Activity 2 Identify management control strengths and weaknesses. (Allow 20 minutes for this activity.)
- Activity 3 Solve a work problem in the area of management control. (Allow 3 hours for this activity.)
- Activity 4 Write a report. (Allow 1 hour for this activity.)

Week 4 Readings

All readings are in *Managing and managing people*, Chapter 4 'Planning and control: making things happen'.

- Reading 1 Making things happen
- Reading 2 Planning and control
- Reading 3 Dealing with complexity

Reading 1

Reading 1, *Making things happen*, in Chapter 4 sets the context for planning and controlling activities. All organisations are involved in transforming inputs into outputs of one kind or another. If the organisation you work for makes products then some resources, such as materials, are 'used up' in this process while others, such as people and buildings, are 'used in' the transformation. This transformation can be hard to see if you work in an organisation that provides information, for example. If you work in a service organisation your core input will be staff and your core activity will be using staff to help, support and provide information to entertain, or feed, clients and customers. The *macro* transformation describes what the organisation does in operational terms, but many *micro* transformations are being performed. We expect that you will be managing one or more of these. As you read *Making things happen* it would be useful to draw two diagrams, the first for the organisation you work for and the second for one of the micro transformations in which you are involved. This will help you to carry out the first activity this week, and provide you with a context for your role and your work in your organisation.

Activity 1

Allow 20 minutes for this activity.

This activity asks you to identify one of the micro operations of your organisation, preferably one that you manage. Using Table 4.1, describe the activity. Then identify the inputs, transformation and outputs. The notes you made while reading *Making things happen* will be useful here. When considering outputs, think about any unwanted ones. List these in Table 4.1. Then consider the impact the activity has. Are there any negative consequences that might need to be addressed at some point in the future? List these too.

Table 4.1 A micro operation: inputs, transformation and outputs

Describe the activity
Inputs
Transformation
Outputs
Negative consequences

This activity is designed to help you focus on a particular activity you are engaged in and to see it in a systematic way.

Activity 1 output

√ • *A completed version of Table 4.1.*

Reading 2

Reading 2, *Planning and control*, in Chapter 4 covers management control and why it is necessary in order for organisations to achieve their aims. In last week's texts, you read an example of problem-solving that concerned an aspect of management control. Planning and control are, at the same time, analytical and social processes involving people. However, they cover the management and control of activities, not the control of people. Understanding this removes many of the negative connotations of the term 'control'. Note that management control is continuous – this explains its other name, 'the control loop'. The idea is that you work round the loop, finally closing it by checking outcomes against planned objectives. As you read, consider the activities in which you are involved and how you manage them. Do you go through all the stages of planning and control? What 'control loop' problems have you encountered recently? Thinking about your own work while you read will help you with Activity 2.

Activity 2

Allow 20 minutes for this activity.

This activity asks you to identify a completed, or nearly completed, task or project which would have been more successful with better control loop processes. Then it asks you to identify which stages of the control loop could have been done better and why – that is, how attention to a particular stage or stages of the control loop could have improved the way in which the task or project was carried out. Finally, it asks you to indicate what you would do differently if you had the opportunity to carry out the task or project again. Use Table 4.2 for your response.

1. *Identify a task.* This should be a small task or project. Problems might be that there were unexpected delays.
2. *What could have been done better?* Using Reading 2, *Planning and control*, in Chapter 4 look at each stage in the control loop and the specific parts of each stage. Consider the way in which each was implemented in the task or project you have identified. Working systematically in this way, you should be able to identify the main areas where improvements could have been made. Note that each stage may have an impact on the next. For example, if staff were not trained then this is likely to have had an impact on whether they were able to meet the performance standards set. In this way you can work out primary causes of any difficulties and separate them from 'symptoms' of the problem that might have been noted later.
3. *List what you would do differently.* Again, we are asking you to examine your own practices and identify ways in which you can improve. In a later activity this week, you will have an opportunity to work on a current workplace task and plan improvements. Good work on the control loop in this first activity will help you to learn well from the later activity.

Table 4.2 What should have happened

Brief description of task or project
Parts of Stage 1 that could have been done better and why
What I would do differently
Parts of Stage 2 that could have been done better and why
What I would do differently
Parts of Stage 3 that could have been done better and why
What I would do differently
Parts of Stage 4 that could have been done better and why?
What I would do differently

As you carried out Activity 2, it is likely that you found reasons why you did not pay more attention to some stages of the control loop or feel that, in the circumstances, things could not have been different. Often these reasons lie in the complexity of managing in an organisation.

Activity 2 output

- *A completed version of Table 4.2.*

Reading 3

Reading 3, *Dealing with complexity*, in Chapter 3 suggests why it might be hard to implement the management control loop at times. The best laid plans can be subject to interference from many quarters – and much will depend on your interpersonal and leadership skills because planning and implementation invariably involve people – the social part of the process. Reading 3 will prepare you for Activity 3, when you will solve a management control loop problem. Your solution to this problem is likely to meet with success if you take into account such factors as insufficient resources, risk and uncertainty, needing a contingency plan (a 'Plan B'), or opposition from others.

Activity 3

Allow 3 hours for this activity.

We now want you to work through a management control problem of your own. It need not be a 'problem' of course. It can be a task or project in which you are currently involved and which is proceeding smoothly. Nonetheless, improvements can always be made and this is an ideal opportunity to identify one or more.

Normally, the identification, analysis and resolution of a workplace problem rely on bringing existing management knowledge to bear on it. In the workplace, even with a good deal of knowledge, you might not actually identify a problem with any refinement until you have analysed it. When you are studying, however, you need guidance to help you identify a problem *as* a particular sort of problem. Further, at this stage in the module, your analysis of situations and issues and your solutions may not cover all aspects of the situation. However, as you progress through the module, you should find that you are able to bring an increasing amount of knowledge to bear on identifying, analysing and resolving problems.

To help you with this first problem-solving activity, we offer a demonstration of the way in which a management control problem was solved in a café.

The illustration of problem-solving that you read last week was quite a complex one involving the management control loop, stakeholders, participation, the potential for conflict, and so on – concepts that you will cover later. The demonstration is simpler, though not only because of this, however: we want you to attend to the process of problem-solving.

The Garden Gate

Patisserie sales at The Garden Gate, a café at a large garden centre, have been falling. A lively meeting place for out-of-town shoppers as well as offering welcome refreshment to garden centre visitors, the café remains lively but customers are more often confining themselves to tea, coffee and other beverages, despite the café's low prices. (The purpose of The Garden Gate is to draw and keep shoppers in the store for long enough to buy, so the café need only return a small profit.) The manager of The Garden Gate walked out of his job three weeks ago and Georgia, a staff supervisor at the garden centre, has been brought in temporarily to run the café until a permanent manager can be found. Georgia takes a keen interest in domestic cooking and seemed an ideal choice.

The Garden Gate's speciality is home-style cakes baked on site by two cooks, often from pre-prepared ingredients in packets. If sales of any product fall significantly, it is replaced by another which the cooks themselves choose from the catalogues of various suppliers of catering ingredients. However, scones – a traditional and popular type of cake in the UK – have never been off the product list at The Garden Gate. Yet sales of these and other cakes are falling. Sales of snacks, while increasing, only just make up the balance and it is clear that, apart from the lunch period, customers prefer cakes to items such as baked potatoes and salad.

The reason for the lack of sales of scones in particular is immediately clear to Georgia. Instead of the scones rising to a good height, they are flat and hard. Georgia discusses the situation with the cook who takes responsibility for the scones. She discovers two things: that the 'scone cook' is unfamiliar with a UK scone and has no idea what scones are supposed to look like; and that the supplier of the pre-prepared scone mix has changed. Over the next week, Georgia discovers that many cakes put on display are not up to standard and the quality is inconsistent day by day. It seems that it is left to the cooks to decide on standards. As she is only the temporary manager, she does not want to upset the cooks – especially if the problem is that the pre-prepared ingredients are at fault.

Georgia also sees that there is a problem with the system for working out how many cakes the cooks should prepare each day. The number depends on sales on the same day the previous week, a system that appeared to work in the past. However, falling cake sales mean that fewer cakes are often made even if the fall in cake sales is due to the poor standard of some individual products the week before. This led to problems the previous week when a new and surprisingly successful almond slice sold out very quickly. Georgia couldn't tell whether this was because the almond slices looked far better in the display cabinet than the other cakes, many of which were left over at the end of the day, or that the almond slices were popular in their own right. At any rate, the situation meant that the cooks did not know how many of each cake type to prepare each day, and overall numbers the same day the previous week were really no guide when a new line was successful.

Over coffee, Georgia mentions the problem to the garden store manager, Gary. Gary asks her for a little time to think about the problem and meets her the following day. Over yet another coffee, he encourages her to take control of the situation and then tells her how she might go about this. What might Gary have said to Georgia?

Problem identification

Georgia knows that there is a problem but doesn't have sufficient knowledge to know what type of problem it is. Gary can see that there seems to be a problem because Georgia has alerted him to the fact. But it is not until she has provided some details to which Gary brings to bear his management knowledge that he knows what sort of problem it is.

In the scenario Georgia is aware that the products are not being produced to a high or consistent standard. Gary, who has more knowledge of management control than Georgia, is familiar with the reasons this might be happening. He tentatively identifies the problem as one of lack of management control as soon as Georgia broaches the problem, but he isn't quite sure until she gives him more information. After that he confidently identifies the problem as one of lack of management control.

When trying to identify a problem, one can know that there is a problem, but not what kind it is until some investigation is done.

Problem analysis

For Gary to positively identify the problem as one of management control he needs to understand the situation more fully. As he listens to Georgia, he maps his knowledge of management control to what she is telling him.

Note that he could make a mistake here. Consider how easy it might be to use and adhere to an idea (a management concept) and try to make the 'evidence' fit! This is an example of a 'known solution, unknown problem' in which insufficient analysis is done.

It is clear to Gary from what Georgia tells him that the only objectives that seemed to have been set are 'make and sell cakes', operationalised as: cook the same number of items as the same day last week, and cook what sells. These objectives are basic but SMART – Specific, Measurable, Agreed, Realistic and Timed.

However, only one standard of performance seems to be in place – performance is measured only by sales. This means that if sales fall, it isn't treated as a management issue. No-one checks whether what the cooks produce is of sufficient quality to be sold: indeed, there are no task performance measures in place so the cooks simply use their own judgement – which clearly is not working in the case of the scones. In short, the cooks are managing themselves and the product lines, and use their own subjective measures of quality. While there are various possible causes of the problem with the scones, Gary felt that the scones had simply highlighted a more fundamental issue – a muddled and insufficiently managed production process.

This is a second example of Gary's bringing his greater knowledge and experience to bear on the problem. While Georgia had been concerned with the system of working out how many cakes to bake each day, Gary is less concerned. He believes that, with a proper management control system in place, such problems should not arise to the same extent.

Problem conclusion

Gary concludes that there is a lack of management control on the basis that there are:

- no clear overall standards
- no task performance measures in place for the cooks
- no task performance measurement
- no proper monitoring and comparison of overall performance with overall objectives (or standards).

Georgia, on the basis of her more limited knowledge and experience, would have concluded that the problem was both one of standards and one of basing the number of cakes to cook each day on ever-diminishing previous sales. From this perspective, the problem looks confusing. She would have muddled through a solution, probably on a trial-and-error basis. Gary, however, can see a much clearer way forward.

Problem solution

Before Gary suggested to Georgia what she might do, he made the assumption that the garden centre was not concerned about pricing or profits, only that it wanted to continue to attract out-of-town shoppers to increase the likelihood of purchases. He also considered the time frame in which the problem needed to be solved: quickly! However, he could see that in the longer term, the garden centre might be persuaded to invest in The Garden Gate and increase profitability in its own right. He put that idea aside, however, reminding himself to think about it later.

When Gary begins to suggest a solution to Georgia, he shows her a decision tree based on the control loop which he prepared to help her understand both the problem better and his proposed solution. The control loop was what came to mind as being useful when Georgia explained the problem. As more of the 'evidence' began to fit what he knew about the control loop, the more convinced he became that it was this sort of problem the café was experiencing. His completed decision tree is shown in Figure 4.1.

Note that Figure 4.1 covers all the aspects of a conventional control loop. The loop is normally shown in the context of projects – initiatives that must be broken down into a number of interrelated tasks. In the case of tasks recurring day to day – that is, situations similar to The Garden Gate, and where improvement is needed rather than a new initiative – emphasis will shift to the relevant parts of the control loop. When you are using a control loop be sure to 'customise it', keeping the key elements but placing the emphasis where you need to.

It is often the case that in solving a problem, more investigation is needed to see whether the solution, or particular aspects of it, will 'work'. However, for the purposes of this demonstration of problem-solving, we will assume that Georgia will seek any additional information as she works through Gary's recommendations later before acting on them. Gary's recommendations to Georgia are as follows, set out in the various stages of the control loop.

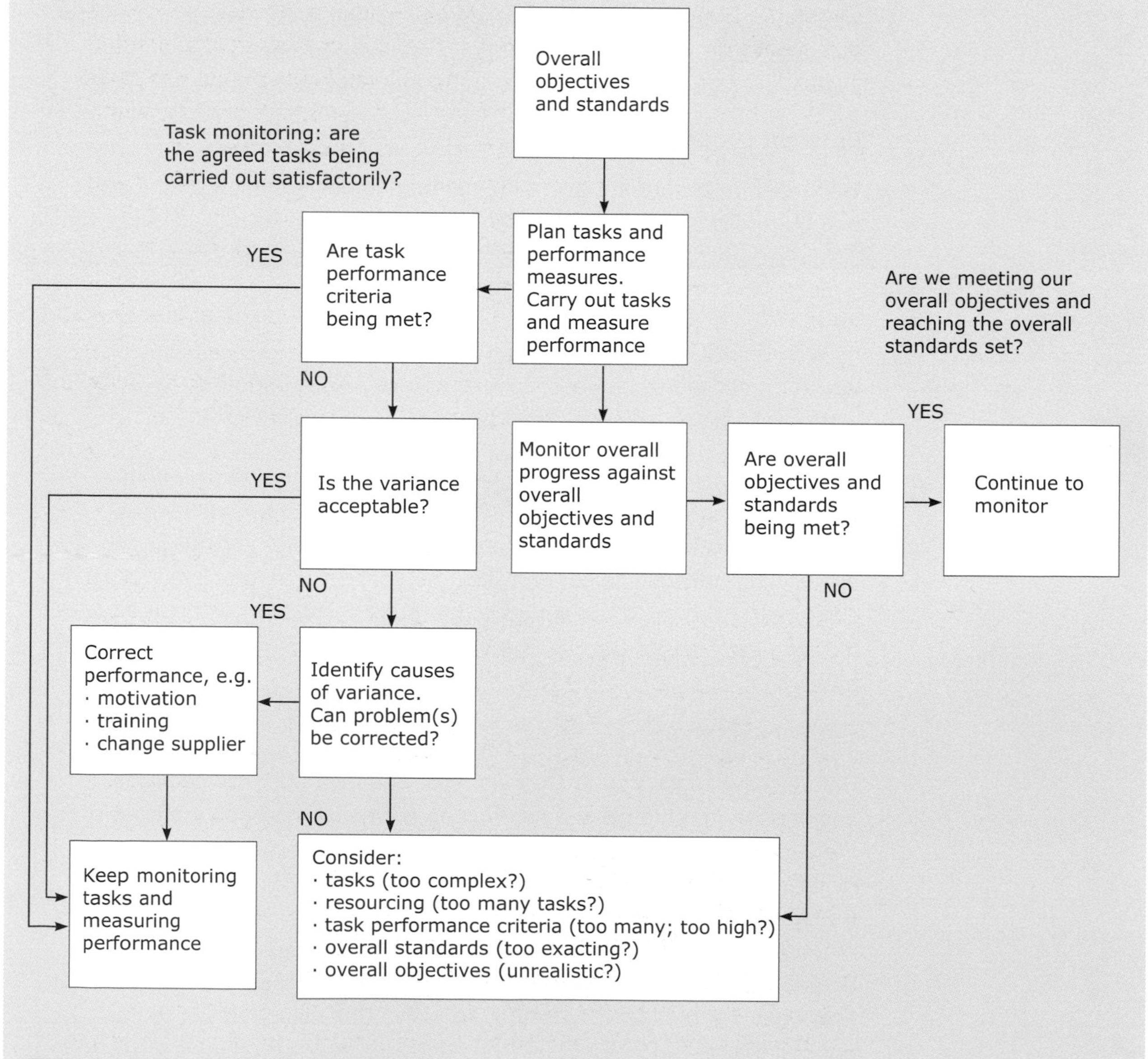

Figure 4.1 Control loop decision tree

1 *Set objectives and performance standards*. The broad objective to make and sell cakes daily, operationalised as a system of making the same number of cakes as were made the same day the previous week, is simple and workable (except for public holidays and special events), provided sales are consistent. The reason that they are not seems to be related to standards of performance at this level and at task level. Overall performance standards need to be established. Gary has a number of ideas for 'resetting' the number and type of cakes that should be cooked each day, but these can wait until cake sales are stable.

The basic standards of performance he suggests are that:

- all products should meet a standard acceptable to customers
- 95% of cakes should be sold by the end of the day
- a variety of cakes should always be offered to customers.

2 *Plan tasks, identify task performance measures and measure task performance*. Gary then moves along his decision tree and recommends that Georgia plans the tasks that will meet the objectives. However, he thinks she should involve the other café staff, including the cooks, in the decision-making and that she should agree task performance measures with the cooks. These task performance measures, of course, need to be derived from and consistent with the overall performance standards. Gary suggests that Georgia carries out visual and taste tests on every batch of cakes before they go on display as a way of ensuring acceptable standards. Any problem with cake quality or inconsistency can be addressed with a little coaching from Georgia, who might also supply photographs of what each cake is supposed to look like and bring in samples from bakeries. Another way of assessing task performance that Gary suggests is for counter staff to talk to customers, gain feedback from questions such as *'Did you find the type of cake you wanted?'* and write it in a daybook. This could supplement cash-till data. The staff themselves might identify good questions to ask as part of their general 'chat' with customers. They might also find more ways of being in contact with customers. Although customers are expected to clear their own tables, staff might clean newly vacated tables near to occupied ones in order to strike up conversation. Georgia herself could be present in the eating area of the café as often as possible to check on customer satisfaction. Finally, Georgia and the staff can decide on the variety of cakes to offer customers. This can be based on customer feedback when sufficient has been gathered; until then the cooks can simply continue with the current range of types. In this way, the performance criteria can be met. Provided the cakes are of an acceptable standard and a variety is offered, and the cooks repeat the successful product lines, the realistic sales target should be met.

3 *Monitor progress and compare actual performance to performance standards*. Gary recommends that Georgia uses the results of her checks, till data and feedback from customers to measure actual performance against the performance standards on a weekly basis. He suggests, too, that she organises a regular weekly staff meeting to communicate her findings to staff, to praise them when they have done well and to discuss improvements with them when necessary.

4 *Act on results of monitoring*. Because Gary can't predict the results of Georgia's monitoring all he is able to do here is to provide encouragement and advice. He tells her not to be afraid to take corrective action if her monitoring shows that standards are not being met. This might involve adjusting the number of cakes made each day depending on sales, and investigating the cause when standards are not met. The standards might be too high given the use of pre-prepared ingredients, which might not result in good quality – a resourcing issue. (The standards might be too high for the cooks themselves but Georgia will have discovered this when checking task performance.)

5 *SMART recommendations*. While making his recommendations to Georgia, Gary has been silently checking that they are SMART – or will be when Georgia turns them into an action plan for herself. He recommends that she makes sure that every part of her plan and expected outcomes are – Specific, Measurable, Agreed, Realistic and Timed. This will be fairly easy because Gary has incorporated all of these, except time, into his recommendations. He suggests that Georgia implements the plan within one week – and offers to be on hand to advise if she needs it.

Advantages, disadvantages and implications

Gary reminds Georgia that his recommendations will not result in a perfect solution. They are, however, cheap to implement and should produce results quickly – these are strengths. The weakness of the solution (though he doesn't mention this to Georgia) is that it depends on her management skills – in particular, her interpersonal skills. She will need to involve all the staff but in particular the cooks and their performance: this part of the solution requires sensitivity, and the morale of the whole staff team is at stake. Georgia will need to ensure that staff 'buy into' the ideas she presents. Gary suggests she introduces the solution as a 'sales recovery plan to ensure the continued success of the business' rather than as an exercise of tighter control, which might lead staff to feel resentful and resist changes to the way things are done.

What Gary also considered but wasn't part of his recommendations

Gary had viewed the problem – and his solution – as relatively well-bounded. He saw no major implications of the solution: it was within the day-to-day work of a manager to exercise such control systems, the plan did not need 'vetting' and it would not require additional resourcing.

However, he had considered that a business can begin to fail for other reasons – a down-turn in consumer spending, for example, or insufficient marketing, or increased competition, or changes in fashion or habits. In other words, there might be fundamental causes of falling sales that poor management control was simply exacerbating. He had thought about possible other causes but could think only of insufficient marketing and a need for refurbishment as possibilities in this case. Further, he knew that, since café sales were not critical to the garden centre, the simplest solution was the best one to try first. This is the kind of contextual and often tacit knowledge that managers bring to the task of problem-solving.

The iterative process and the role of knowledge and experience

Gary had an instinctive feeling about the solution to the problem that seemed familiar to him. But he needed to be sure that the problem was the one he thought it was. Thus, in a sense, he was working on several aspects of problem-solving iteratively rather than moving through the process step by step. Even when he arrived at a potential solution, he still checked it against his original analysis and conclusions.

Gary analysed the problem and made recommendations on the basis of the information Georgia gave him. This information was provided in the scenario but normally would have to be discovered by investigation, observation and seeking information from those involved. What questions you ask, what you investigate or observe will be influenced by the kind of problem you think exists. It is possible to look in quite the wrong place unless one keeps an open mind. However, as an experienced and knowledgeable manager presented with a relatively simple and familiar problem, Gary was able to work through it quite easily. He was also able to include in his recommendations what he knows about the importance of communication and involving staff (which the control loop doesn't tell you!).

If Georgia had been solving this problem with only a text on the management control loop to help her, she might have tried to work through the problem-solving process systematically. She might have felt that it was somehow wrong to work backwards and forwards through the various 'stages' of problem-solving and to seek more information as ideas occurred to her about the nature of the problem itself and whether a potential solution might work.

However, if she had then written down what the problem was and what she intended to do about it, it would have appeared that she'd worked through it in serial fashion. In other words, writing it down afterwards makes problem-solving look far easier than it is! Using an iterative process is perfectly normal in complex situations, however experienced and knowledgeable a person might be.

Now identify a management control problem you are currently experiencing, or have experienced recently. Alternatively, identify a task or project in which you are involved that you want to use as an opportunity to improve your management control skills. Make sure the problem or task is well 'bounded' or it may be too big for this first exercise in problem-solving. If you resolved the problem at the time, don't worry – a comparison between how you resolved it then and how you might resolve it now will be useful.

To identify the problem, and work through it until you have a solution, you may need some of the tools and techniques set out in 'Tools and techniques' in *Managing and managing people*. Useful tools include:

- systems maps
- fishbone diagrams
- multiple-cause diagrams
- network analysis.

Select what seems to be useful but don't spend too long using a tool or technique that isn't helping you.

Now work through the problem, going through the structured problem-solving process using the textbook example. Remember, it doesn't matter if you work on several aspects of the problem at once: possible solutions might occur to you while you are still analysing the problem; equally, a solution might have to be abandoned because you suddenly think of an aspect of the problem you forgot to analyse. Real problem-solving is invariably more iterative than any example or demonstration can convey.

Step 1 Identifying the problem and describing it

First, think about a significant task or project that you planned and carried out, but which caused you problems. Then consider the following questions to help you identify and describe the problem, understand to whom it was a problem and why, and recognise any other impacts:

- Who was involved and what were their roles, perspectives and capabilities? In what ways did these people have an influence on the task?
- What was your role?
- Were there other people who had an influence, e.g. your own line manager?
- Did you begin the task with any obvious staff, organisational constraints or potential difficulties, e.g. budgetary constraints, new, untrained staff?
- What issues arose as you carried out the project or task?
- What were the effects of these issues on the task or project, on the people involved in it, on you, on others in the organisation and the organisation (or parts of it)?

Try to use management concepts and ideas as you think about the questions. Answering them should allow you to identify and describe the problem. You won't need all the detail you noted but it is likely to be useful later.

Step 2 Analysing the problem

Now begin to analyse the problem. An appropriate method for a management control problem is to apply the control loop. Do this stage by stage in order to analyse the problem.

Consider Stage 1, *The objectives*. Were they realistic given the context, circumstances and resources?

Consider Stage 2, *Planning, identification of markers and the carrying out/ commencement of tasks*. What problems arose here and why?

Consider Stage 3, *Monitoring progress*. How effectively were you able to do this? What difficulties did you experience and why? What did the monitoring reveal?

Consider Stage 4, *Acting on the results of monitoring*. Did any actions result from monitoring, and if so what were they? Were there tasks that needed to be adjusted, redone or abandoned? Were the objectives revised in any way, and why? Note that the perspectives and capabilities of others involved in the task, or those who influenced it at any stage, are likely to have a bearing on your answers to these questions, as well as the expectations of these people and others, and the general expectations of your part of your organisation.

Answering these questions should help you to analyse the problem. Note how you have used a management concept to help you to do this. This is exactly how we expect you to apply module concepts when you carry out activities in this module. Customised diagrams can also help you to analyse a problem and show other people how you analysed it. This is important when you share your findings formally with others.

Now consider whether, when you answered these questions, you had to make any assumptions. For example, you may have had to assume that the training staff received was adequate, or that your own expectations were realistic.

Refer briefly to any gaps in your analysis. If you identified any (for example, aspects of the problem you were unable to analyse because the information was not available or too expensive to collect) then specify what they are; again, this is important when you show your findings to others. Identifying any gaps will also help you to assess, in Step 3, how confident you are in your conclusion.

Step 3 Drawing a conclusion

Draw together the elements of your analysis into a conclusion. Try to step back from the detail of your analysis: make sense of your findings and develop an overview. You may have analysed what appeared to be a muddle, element by element, but when you stand back it may be clear that many of the elements were symptoms of a single problem, such as unclear objectives. Try to interpret your findings rather than just list them. Make sure that your conclusion is drawn from your analysis and covers important causes of the problem and the significant findings. Make sure it does not contain any additional information: if it does, it may be because you forgot something in your analysis, or that you're including elements of the solution.

Step 4 Recommendations

Now you have reached the solution phase. First, you will need to explain what your solution aims to achieve – the criteria for a solution. Will it resolve the problem completely or simply reduce it to an acceptable level? Will the solution be a short-term or long-term remedy? Are major changes possible, or does your solution aim to make as little change as possible? Will your solution address only the problem you have analysed or do you want it to have wider application or be system-changing? Does the solution need to reflect financial or other constraints such as resources, skills and timescales?

When considering your criteria recognise any organisational constraints. Bear in mind that potential solutions to the problem need to be acceptable to those involved, to those who have an interest in it and to the organisation in general. Solutions often need to 'fit' what seems normal and usual to an organisation and its staff. However, even under such constraints you can explore innovative solutions.

When you have set out your criteria for a solution, you can then work out how you will achieve the solution – one that will meet the criteria. Your potential solution, or solutions, will not be drawn from your conclusions but must address the conclusions. For example, if the problem is that monitoring revealed problems which required an adjustment to a task, but that this adjustment could not be made because Person X did not have the skills, a possible solution might be to adjust, with agreement, the roles of people rather than to train Person X if Person X is about to retire and is not motivated to improve their skills, or if time is too short.

As you consider possible solutions, you are likely to find that they will change and that you will abandon some possibilities. Do this using the 'Framework for comparing options and making choices' in *Managing and managing people*, Chapter 3.

When you have achieved a good, practical and perhaps innovative solution, set it out as a series of recommendations. Ensure that the recommendations are SMART – Specific, Measurable, Agreed, Realistic and Timed. In the case of 'Agreed', say whose agreement will be needed and the likelihood of obtaining it. If you have had to make further assumptions, say what these are.

Use module concepts and customised diagrams where appropriate. Consider the module themes. Is your solution ethical? Will it lead to more efficient use of resources? Will it reduce carbon emissions?

Step 5 Advantages, disadvantages and implications

A number of advantages and disadvantages – strengths and weaknesses – are likely to have emerged in Step 4. If not, consider them now and say what they are. For example, your solution directly addresses the problem, but it relies on Person Y's willingness to accept an adjustment to their role or getting agreement to delay the task deadline by one week.

Then consider the implications of your solution. Your preferred solution may raise further questions. For example, Person X may need to undergo training; this may require funding and there may be a need for another person to cover while they are away. If the implications of your solution are too expensive or complex, you may need to review it.

Say how disadvantages or negative implications might be mitigated – if they can be.

A common difficulty in problem-solving is that a problem turns out to be less 'bounded' than you previously thought, so the solution has implications for other activities or other parts of the organisation. The realisation that there is a major implication of this kind should alert you to the probability that your solution may not succeed and you may need to return to a prior stage in the problem-solving process. An example of such an implication would be realising that extending the task deadline by one week would ultimately have a major and unacceptable impact elsewhere in the organisation.

Now complete Table 4.3, using the notes you have made.

Table 4.3 A management control problem

Problem identification and description
Analysis
Conclusion to the analysis
Recommendations
Advantages, disadvantages and implications

Congratulations on completing your first full problem-based activity. It may have been a satisfying experience to see how you can manage something better. Equally, you are likely to have identified demands and constraints that restrict and influence your choices. You may have experienced tension between what you would like to do and what is possible. Your solution may not be the one that, in ideal circumstances, you would choose. But that doesn't matter: a 'good enough' solution that works for *your* workplace context has a high chance of success.

Activity 3 output

- *A completed version of Table 4.3.*

Activity 4

Allow 1 hour for this activity.

As a manager you will be familiar with the request to 'write a short report'. Table 4.3 doesn't serve this purpose. How do you turn the contents of Table 4.3 into a form that your own line manager would expect? Now you will do just that – turn your work from Activity 3 into a report format as if to your line manager, putting the text you inserted in Table 4.3 where indicated in Table 4.4, which is based on a classic report format. Below Table 4.4 are some notes to help you decide what to include in each section of the report. More information about the report format can be found in *The Manager's Good Study Guide* in 'Writing reports', together with guidance on identifying your sources of information in 'Citing and referencing'. Note, however, that in this module when you write reports you do not need to think about how many report sections or subsections you need or what type of content to put in them. Appendices, which are the final component of a report, have been omitted as you will not need them for activity outputs.

Your completed report should be about 750 words long, excluding the cover page, contents page, references, any diagrams and any appendices. (Tables are always included in word counts.) Your report is likely to be more formal and structured than the output for Activity 3.

Table 4.4 Report

Cover page
Summary
Contents
Introduction
Analsis
Conclusions to the analysis
Recommendations
Advantages, disadvantages and implications
References

What to put in the various sections

Cover page. Include the title of the report, addressee(s), author and date.

Summary. The summary is often called an executive summary, and allows a reader to absorb quickly the main points you make in your report. This releases your readers from uncertainty straight away – but you want them to read the report, so try to make the summary interesting. Use numbered and indented paragraphs if you wish. If you do, use them throughout the report.

Report writers often write the summary last. It is often easier to summarise a report after you have written it and included the detail in the body of the report.

Contents. List each the title of each section and subsection of the report (and section and subsection numbers if you are using a numerical system), including the Introduction. Insert page numbers if appropriate.

Introduction. Introduce your report. The Introduction prepares the reader for what is to come. If you are writing the report for a person who is not familiar with your part of the organisation you will need to include a brief description – giving some of its key features and stating your role.

Then you need to identify and describe the problem that prompted the report. You will also need to set out to whom the problem is important and why (and any other impacts), and the purpose of the report. The Introduction should also state the scope (that is, the boundaries of the matter addressed) and limitations of the investigation you carried out, together with (briefly) the sources and methods you used for investigation. Include a summary of your findings.

An appropriate place to start in the case of The Garden Gate is to identify the problem as a management control issue, in particular, quality control. Then describe it by stating what led you to realise there was a problem: for example, falling and inconsistent sales of cakes, its speciality. Next, state to whom this is a problem and why. In a situation such as The Garden Gate the problem would not only affect customers and the organisation in general but also the catering staff, and those who manage them, as a result of the customer complaints and efforts to halt falls in sales.

The purpose of the report is to set out a set of recommendations, or actions taken, to resolve the problem. In describing the scope of the report you might state that your investigation was confined purely to quality, or supply (production), rather than 'demand' involving customers' wants and needs. In the case of The Garden Gate, the methods of investigation are probably too limited and informal to mention in the Introduction, but this wouldn't be the case if the investigation had involved staff interviews, or gathering feedback from consumers using questionnaires.

Set out the main assumptions it has been necessary for you to make. For example, if the solution to the problem involves a small cost, you may have made the assumption that the benefits of the solution outweigh this cost and it is therefore likely to be acceptable.

Show that you have recognised any issues of ethics, sustainability or climate change (the module themes) in the situation being addressed. You might state, for example, that your solution is fair to staff, has the potential to improve skills and morale, and will not lead to an increase in material waste. Alternatively, state that such issues are addressed in the report (but don't forget to deal with them). More information about these themes can be found in the Module Guide.

Analysis. This will be your first main section of the report. If the problem is a complex one, then it is useful to begin by providing some detail on the aspects of it that you will be analysing. Then set out your analysis. In the case of The Garden Gate, the analysis might explore how the management control system currently in place appears to result in falling and inconsistent sales.

Use module concepts, customised diagrams and module themes as appropriate. It is often helpful to say why a management concept is relevant in your analysis. As you become more experienced at using module concepts you may also find that they have limitations. Again, it is useful to mention these limitations when they constrain your analysis of a particular aspect of a problem. For example, the control loop does not reflect the difficulties of setting standards or the difficulties in persuading individuals to accept changes in standards. That allows you easily to introduce and analyse these aspects of the problem, while demonstrating your critical thinking to the reader. This will help your report to sound authoritative.

Take time to consider issues of ethics, sustainability and climate change. You may be surprised to find how are relevant they are, both in your analysis and in your recommendations. This will demonstrate the thoroughness of your thinking.

Mention any gaps in your analysis. While drawing attention to such gaps may not seem to be sensible, revealing that you are aware of any shortcomings will demonstrate the quality of your thinking. As a result you will inspire confidence in the readers of your report.

Set out any relevant assumptions you have had to make in your analysis. Stating assumptions, like identifying gaps in your analysis, also reveals the quality of your thinking.

Conclusions to the analysis. This part of the report will be a subsection to the first main section. It is important to note that conclusions to an analysis are not a conclusion to the report as a whole.

Ensure that there is a correspondence between your conclusions and the summary. Don't introduce any new information – your conclusion needs to be drawn from your analysis. The main mistake students make when writing conclusions is adding new information and discussion. If you have missed something important, then you will need to return to your analysis. Another mistake – both in the analysis and conclusions – is to include recommendations. These come later.

Provide an overview and set out the important causes of the problem and significant features of your analysis.

Recommendations. This part of the report will be the second main section. First set out your criteria for a solution – what your solution needs to achieve to resolve the problem. Then set out your solution as a set of SMART recommendations. Make sure that they meet the criteria and address the problem. If you have had to make further assumptions, say what these are.

Recognise any organisational constraints in your criteria for a solution and in your recommendations. Use module concepts and diagrams where necessary, and refer to module themes of ethics, sustainability and climate where these are relevant.

Advantages, disadvantages and implications. This part of your report will be a subsection to the second main section. Use it to comment on the advantages and disadvantages – the strengths and weaknesses – of your recommendations. When you do this, you are commenting on the feasibility of your recommendations, that is, how easy or otherwise it will be to implement them, problems that might arise or benefits that they might bring. You might also mention any organisational constraints you may encounter if your recommendations are implemented. You may need to set out how any disadvantages might be mitigated. If you make recommendations, make sure they are SMART.

Also cover the implications of your recommendations. Again, you may find that you need to set out further recommendations for mitigating the effects of a negative implication. It is a matter of judgement whether recommendations for reducing disadvantages and negative implications should be integrated into the main recommendations, but in this module, they are included in a subsection to make the report clearer for readers.

End on a positive note – you are trying to sell these recommendations to someone, probably your boss!

References. List the sources of information you used in your report. References should be of a uniform style and follow the Harvard system, set out in *The Manager's Good Study Guide* in 'Citing and referencing', which covers: books (including module textbooks), contributions in a book, articles in a journal, newspaper articles, publications from an organisation, web pages, diagrams and other media. Another source of information is the *Assessment booklet*.

It is good practice to include a file reference so that the report can be easily retrieved from an archive – your own, or that of your organisation. It is also usual to sign the end of the report (before the appendices and references) but you won't be able to do that for this activity.

Appendices are not included in the report format provided here. They can be a useful way of including additional information, such as sales figures or organisational structure, to support statements you have made in the report. However, your report should be capable of being read without the appendices, which provide only supplementary information. You may find appendices useful in your TMAs and EMA reports for the purposes of presentation but note that material in appendices does not attract marks.

Activity 4 should familiarise you with the structure of a report and what kind of information fits into the different sections. While it may have seemed a little like completing a jigsaw puzzle, your learning from it will be useful when you write your TMAs and EMA.

Activity 4 output

- *A completed version of Table 4.4.*

Week 4 activity outputs

1. A completed version of Table 4.1.
2. A completed version of Table 4.2.
3. A completed version of Table 4.3.
4. A completed version of Table 4.4.

Learning outcomes

After completing this set of activities and readings you should be able to:

- understand your role in the operations of your organisation
- understand the process of management control
- use the problem-solving process
- understand how problem-solving tools and techniques can be used
- understand the structure and content of a formal report
- compile a report.

Week 5 Managing information

Introduction

'I wish I had been given that information before starting the task.'

'I received all the data on X but it's difficult to use in this form.'

'Why doesn't that information go to George before Marie; he doesn't get it in time to use it properly.'

'I've no idea why I receive these reports – I don't need them.'

These are typical statements. Indeed, you may have made similar ones recently. All concern problems with information. Information has a vital function for managers because managerial decisions and actions are only as good as the information on which they are based and how that information is used. This is why managing information and information flows is a core management skill. Two important types of management decisions concern monitoring, which you considered last week, and evaluation, a topic to be covered at the end of this module. Our coverage of the management of information deals with more than the kind of information you might need for monitoring activities: we consider what information is, how it flows, the qualities and costs of good information, information requirements and, finally, how to investigate and improve a communication system.

Week 5 Activities

- Activity 1 Identify the main categories of information that you deal with at work, with examples. (Allow 30 minutes for this activity.)
- Activity 2 Assess the qualities of the information in the examples you gave of the information you receive, need and provide. (Allow 20 minutes for this activity.)
- Activity 3 Identify an information system for an activity that you manage and specify the inputs, transformation processes and outputs. (Allow 30 minutes for this activity.)
- Activity 4 Write a report on an information system that you have identified and analysed and in which you set out your conclusions and recommendations for any improvements that can be made. (Allow 4 hours for this activity.)

Week 5 Readings

All readings are in *Managing and managing people*, Chapter 5 'Managing information'.

- Reading 1 What do we mean by information?
- Reading 2 The qualities and cost of good information
- Reading 3 Information requirements
- Reading 4 Management information systems
- Reading 5 Improving your information management
- Reading 6 What you need when you need it: dealing with information overload (optional)

Activity 1

Allow 30 minutes for this activity.

In this activity, you will identify some of the data and information that you deal with in the course of your job. Many managers may not recognise that managing information is a central focus of their jobs, even though they may spend more time dealing with information than anything else. Activity 1 is designed to help you identify some of the main categories of data and information that surround you at work. This will help when you read the various texts on information; then you will know that the content really does apply to you.

Use Table 5.1 for the task. Leave the final column blank. You will complete this column in Activity 2.

List three examples of each of the following kinds of data and information you deal with in the course of carrying out your job:

- Information you receive regularly from others (for example, monthly budget printouts from your finance department, data from your personnel department).
- Information you need to collect (for example, how many clients you can expect next week, how many companies are waiting for product deliveries that are overdue, how much leave someone is due).
- Information from external sources (for example, guidelines from professional bodies, reports from bodies such as the Audit Commission in the UK or a trade association for your sector).
- Information you pass on to others (for example, safety bulletins, memos from your manager about new developments or other matters, complaints by customers or service users).

Against each of your examples, make a brief note of how it is normally communicated to you or how you communicate it to others (for example, word-of-mouth, notice board, email, internal or external post, intranet, internet).

Make sure you have given a reasonable overall picture of some of the main sources of information for you at work.

Table 5.1 Information handling

Information I receive regularly from others Example 1 Example 2 Example 3	**How the information is communicated**	**Overall quality of information**
Information I need to be able to find out Example 1 Example 2 Example 3	**How the information is communicated**	**Overall quality of information**
Information from external sources Example 1 Example 2 Example 3	**How the information is communicated**	**Overall quality of information**
Information I need to pass on to others Example 1 Example 2 Example 3	**How the information is communicated**	**Overall quality of information**

Before you carried out this activity, would you have considered handling information to be an important part of your job? The activity focussed on relatively formal information. As you carried it out, it probably occurred to you how much more information you handle in the course of your work and how informally some of it can be received or disseminated. Information you need to pass on to others could have included: tell Sue about the presentation next month, she'll want to know it's happening. Such information could have been passed on when, fortuitously, you were both walking down the corridor at the same time. As we will see, such information counts as information, just as informal methods of delivering it constitute part of the flow of information.

Activity 1 output

- *Table 5.1 with columns 1 and 2 completed.*

Readings 1 and 2

Start with Reading 1, *What do we mean by information?*, in Chapter 5. You should be able to find connections between what you did in Activity 1, the key points in the reading and what you do as a manager. Note the difference between 'data' and 'information'. As you read, you might consider how the same data can be interpreted differently by different people with different interests in your organisation, or your part of it. Also consider the different groups whose information needs you have to consider in your work as a manager. This is likely to be important when you come to Activity 4.

Then move on to Reading 2, *The qualities and cost of good information*, in Chapter 5. There are, or will have been, times when the information that you or members of your team receive is substantial but is not 'good enough'. It is not fit for purpose in some way. Good information has particular qualities. The reading sets out 10 criteria on which to judge information, its value in terms of opportunity costs, access to information and protection of it.

Activity 2

Allow 20 minutes for this activity.

This activity asks you to rate the qualities of the information of which you gave examples in Activity 1 – examples of information you receive regularly, information you need to be able to find out, information from external sources and information you pass on to others. To do this, consider the 10 criteria on which to judge information and rate the information indicated in each example. In each case, give it a score from 1–3, where 1 is weak and 3 is strong. Then record your scores in Table 5.1. This activity is designed to encourage your awareness and understanding of the qualities of information and what 'fitness for purpose' means. It is also designed to prepare you for Activity 4.

When considering the qualities of the information in your examples, you may have identified some quite specific differences in the information you receive, want or pass on as a manager. How did you rate the information you pass on? If you don't receive feedback on the information from the recipients, you may have considered that it would be useful to seek it.

Activity 2 output

- *A completed version of Table 5.1.*

Readings 3 and 4

Reading 3, *Information requirements*, in Chapter 5 addresses the issue of what information is for. Managers mainly use information when making decisions, primarily those involving monitoring processes and evaluating effectiveness. You might like to reflect on the information requirements that you encountered when dealing with management control and, in particular, monitoring in Week 4. The reading covers sources of information, types of information and appropriate information. The latter is of considerable importance when providing information to those outside the organisation – customers, clients, consumers and the general public. The needs of these groups require consideration.

Reading 4, *Management information systems*, in Chapter 5 considers information flows: what information, from where, for what purpose and to whom. You will encounter again the transformational model (inputs–transformation–outputs) in the context of information. Activity 3 uses this model and it would be useful to try to apply this model to one or more of your workplace activities as you read.

Activity 3

Allow 30 minutes for this activity.

Identify an activity you carry out and work out the information system that underpins it, based on the data–transformation process–information model in the text you have just read. The system you choose may or may not be an electronic system.

Then, using Table 5.2, identify:

1 The data inputs.

2 The information outputs.

3 The processes that transform the data inputs into outputs.

4 The nature of the feedback loop that ensures the information generated is accurate and is helpful to those receiving it.

Use the illustration in *Management information systems* in Chapter 5 to guide you.

Table 5.2 Inputs, outputs and processes

Brief description of activity
Data inputs
Information outputs
Processes to transform data inputs into information outputs
The feedback loop

How difficult you found this activity will depend on your workplace context. Some inputs, outputs and processes are very clearly defined or visible in some organisations or parts of it. In others, these elements can be rather harder to identify. The activity should have helped you to see yourself, and others involved in the activity you identified, as part of a transformational system – an information one. This will help you in Activity 4.

Activity 3 output

- *A completed version of Table 5.2.*

Reading 5

Reading 5, *Improving your information management*, in Chapter 5 brings all the material from the previous readings together into a practical, step-by-step process. In Activity 4 you will follow this to review the qualities of the information and/or information flows over which you have influence and then plan improvements or solve an information problem. Note that the step-by-step process provides techniques for 'problem-finding' as well as identifying causes of existing problems. Make sure you understand each step. If you don't, then refer back to the previous readings in which the concepts used in each step were set out more fully.

Activity 4

Allow 4 hours for this activity.

In this activity you will identify and plan improvements to an information issue that you are experiencing in your own workplace. First you will need to identify an information issue and consider it in terms of the transformational model, and, if it is helpful, an information flow diagram. The problem may be a service or activity that is being adversely affected by the information quality, flow or processes, or human resource elements (awareness, skills). Or it could be one that is adversely affected by organisational structures that make it hard for people to access the information they need (creating 'bottlenecks' in the information system). It may be a system that is apparently working relatively well. In this case you will be identifying where and how it can be improved. Alternatively, there may be an obvious problem with the system, one that needs to be remedied. Try to choose an information issue over which you have influence and which is well-bounded. As all information systems in an organisation are likely to link to one another at an organisational level (as ideally they should!), you might like to select an activity in which giving and receiving information is carried out relatively informally within your work group. You should try to do this if you have no influence over the quality or flow of formal information in your work activities.

Follow the steps set out in Reading 5. These will guide you through Activity 4 systematically from diagnosing a weakness in a system to planning the implementation of a solution. Make notes as you carry out each step and then, using these notes, create a short report. Remember, it is wise to talk to the information users both when analysing an information system and when working out how to improve it. You may want to carry out at least part of this task in your workplace; indeed, it may be possible for you to carry it out as part of your work.

A report format is provided for this activity in Table 5.3. The report template is a shortened version of the one shown in *The Manager's Good Study Guide* 'Writing reports'. You may find it helpful to refer back to the guidance provided in Week 4 Activity 4 to ensure that you include the appropriate information in each part of the report.

Your completed report should be about 750 words excluding the cover page, summary, contents page, any diagrams and any appendices. Tables are always included in the word count.

Table 5.3 Information report

Cover page
Summary
Contents
Introduction
Analysis
Conclusions to the analysis
Recommendations
Advantages, disadvantages and implications
References

This activity may have been a challenging one. It is likely that you found that no information system is bounded: what is an output in one system is an input to another and a change in one place has implications in several other places. This is especially the case when data are used for more than one purpose. However, it may also have been very satisfying. It is satisfying to know that there are times when we can see how we can make improvements. If you found that there was little you could do about the situation, there is some satisfaction in that too. There are times when we have to accept the way things are because to change them requires a major change. At least we know why the system is as it is.

Activity 4 output

- *A completed version of Table 5.3.*

Reading 6 (optional)

Reading 6, *What you need when you need it: dealing with information overload*, in Chapter 5 contains a series of useful tips on avoiding information overload, which happens when we receive far more information than we can deal with. Many of the tips concern informal information and use practices from time management as well as information handling. Select some to put into practice today.

Week 5 activity outputs

1. A completed version of Table 5.1 incorporating outputs from Activities 1 and 2.
2. A completed version of Table 5.2.
3. A completed version of Table 5.3.

Learning outcomes

After completing this set of activities and readings you should be able to:

- understand and demonstrate understanding of the qualities of information, its value, access to it and protection of it
- understand and demonstrate understanding of the information needed for organisations and managers for decision-making
- understand and demonstrate understanding of information requirements for decision-making
- understand and demonstrate understanding of the information needs of those outside the organisation
- understand and demonstrate understanding of information flows and systems
- know how to improve information flow for an activity in which you are involved.

Week 6 TMA 01 preparation

In this week you will prepare your TMA 01.

Week 7 Understanding people at work

Introduction

You have now considered what managers do and have looked at developing some of the skills needed to do it. Now we move on to considering other people – the resource used by managers to achieve organisational objectives. We present what managers need to understand if they are to get the job done effectively and efficiently, while maintaining a positive climate and staff satisfaction. There have probably been times in your own work life when your organisation did not provide you with what you expected. At other times you may have felt that your personal values have been challenged by what you were asked to do. Most of us have had times at work when we have felt highly motivated or demotivated. When this happened, was your work performance affected in any way? If so, you will already know that an understanding of people's beliefs, values, motivation and expectations is important if people are to work effectively to meet the organisation's and their own needs which may be different. Beliefs, values, motivations for going to work every day, and the expectations of the organisation, may differ among the individuals you work with and may also be different from your own. Thus, you will need to explore these in various ways when necessary and appropriate.

The first reading this week describes ways of understanding people at work. The focus then moves to the most popular Western theories on motivation at work and the relevance of these theories to managers in understanding and working with the people they manage. The key theory is the Psychological Contract which is very useful for the practising manager. Expectancy Theory considers the matches and mismatches of expectation between an individual and the organisation. The main activity this week is problem-based.

Week 7 Activities

- Activity 1 Identify your reasons for doing the job you do. (Allow 1 hour for this activity.)
- Activity 2 Either analyse and plan how to resolve a motivation issue in your workplace, or write a review of your management practices with regard to motivation, and how you will change your practice. (Allow 3–4 hours for this activity.)

Week 7 Readings

All readings are in *Managing and managing people*, Chapter 6 'Understanding people at work'.

- Reading 1 Individuals and organisations
- Reading 2 The Psychological Contract
- Reading 3 Expectancy Theory
- Reading 4 Other theories of motivation

Activity 1

Allow 1 hour for this activity.

Before you start this week's reading consider your own reasons for doing the job you do. This will help you to think about why you do the job you do (and not others). It will also help you see the match between what you expect from work and what the organisation expects of you. If you are clear about your own beliefs, motivations and expectations, then it will be easier for you to consider those of the people you work with.

To help get you started, write down your responses to the questions below. The questions refer to beliefs, values and motivations, which are often difficult to identify because people define them differently. Here are some basic definitions.

- *Beliefs* are ideas, propositions or statements that you consider to be true; for example, work is the means by which most people acquire sufficient money to live.
- *Values* are beliefs in which a person has an *emotional investment*; for example, it is right for people to work to acquire sufficient money to live. This may imply another belief, such as it is not right for people to acquire money by criminal activity. Values are sometimes referred to as attitudes – a combination of beliefs and feelings and evaluation. It is possible to hold beliefs and values without acting on them. For example, we may disagree with taxation laws but nonetheless comply with them.
- *Motivation* is what makes a person act. At a basic level, we seek food when we are hungry. Similarly, if working brings benefits such as income to support the family, self-esteem, intellectual stimulation and social benefits, then we will be motivated to work.

You may find other, more complex definitions but these will be sufficient for you to carry out Activity 1.

The questions below assume that you are employed by an organisation (and not running your own business, in self-employment or occupied in some other way). You may need to adapt the questions to cover your particular circumstances.

1 *What beliefs and values do you hold which affect your choice of work and how you do it?* For example, do you work primarily to earn money, or because what you do fits with your personal values, such as making a

contribution to society? One approach to these questions is to ask: Why don't I give up work? Why do I do *this* type of work and not another? Why do I work for *this* organisation and not another?

2 *What does your organisation expect of you?* For example, does your organisation and/or your manager expect you to be committed, always to be ready to meet new challenges, or to work hard to meet difficult deadlines even if this means disruption to family life, or more pressure and stress?

3 *What do you expect from your organisation?* For example, do you expect the organisation to trust you and to be fair about weekend work?

4 *How well do your expectations match those of the organisation you work for?* Are there any mismatches?

5 *What motivates you to go to work each day and to put effort into your work?* This is similar to Question 1 but concerns motives rather than values or beliefs. Recall that one can have values and beliefs but not act on them. For example, you may have some negative beliefs about the outputs of your organisation, perhaps as a result of your political or religious beliefs. But you may still be motivated at work as a result of a deep interest in the content of your professional work.

6 *What demotivates you at work?* For example, would not receiving a pay rise, a promotion or training make you feel that you are not being rewarded sufficiently for your efforts? Does the organisation's attitude towards employees, or the communication climate, make you less inclined to work hard? Does your line manager show a lack of trust in you that makes you feel less confident and less willing to act on your own initiative?

This activity is likely to have been challenging. You may have identified a belief only to find that it is based on a deeper one – a 'core' belief. You may also have found that what motivates you to work (and at work) is not wholly related to your beliefs and values. Some of your motivation may be to do with what appear to be basic needs, while some may be based on your hopes of achieving certain things. Looking at why we do what we do is complex and our beliefs, values and motivations are not necessarily clear to us; we will not be aware of all of them. Thus, we can expect that when we try to discover what motivates the people we manage, it will be difficult. Direct approaches such as asking them may not be productive (and may be intrusive). Their behaviour and the reasons they give for their feelings may be all you have to work with. So, if you found the activity difficult you will have gained knowledge of just why it is so difficult to gain a deep understanding of other people at work.

At this point it is useful to see how your own beliefs, values and motivations differ from – or are similar to – those of other people. First, summarise your responses to the questions posed. There is no template for your responses so create your summary in a Word file.

Then select the responses that you are willing to share with other students in your tutor group. Post this selection to the Week 7 activity forum in a message of not more than 200 words. Read the postings of at least two other students. Then, in a Word file, write three key points on the similarities and differences between the beliefs, values and motivations they have chosen to reveal and your own. You should not be surprised to find differences between individuals, particularly if your fellow students work for very different types of organisation and if a number of cultures are represented in your tutor group. Equally, you should not be surprised to find similarities: few people can afford not to work for money, although this may not be the primary or only motivation. People's other motivations may be the more interesting ones, and different from your own.

Activity 1 outputs

- *A summary of your responses to questions.*
- *A contribution to the Week 7 activity forum.*
- *Three key points on the similarities and differences between your own (selected) beliefs, values and motivations to (and at) work and those of at least two other students.*

Reading 1

Now read *Individuals and organisations* in Chapter 6. This focusses on behaviour in the workplace and the different values and beliefs people hold. It then considers how these might have influenced the type of job or career they have chosen. Which of Schein's concept of 'career anchors' best fits your current priorities? Can you match some of the other career anchors to people in your work group or to yourself some time ago?

Readings 2, 3 and 4

These readings in Chapter 6 are on motivation and cover four theories. Two of these theories described in *The Psychological Contract* and *Expectancy Theory* are more useful than the other two theories covered in the third reading, *Other theories of motivation*. The readings offer you the opportunity to see what can be learned from them in order to understand issues of motivation within the workplace. *The Psychological Contract* focusses on 'content' theories of motivation and on the match between what an individual expects from an organisation and what the organisation expects of the individual. It has practical value for the manager because breaches of this unstated contract can be explored (and anticipated) as part of day-to-day management without the need for intrusive discussions with an individual about their motives. As you read, consider your own expectations and those of your organisation. You may find that you had expectations you were not fully aware of. *Expectancy Theory* placed emphasis on the link between effort and reward, and what types of reward may be effective motivators. Note, however, that what one person finds rewarding may not be rewarding to another person: the manager will have to discover this. Consider what about your own job is rewarding 'in itself' – that is, which rewards come with the job – and which others need to be provided by the organisation to maintain your motivation. The last reading, *Other theories of motivation,* covers older theories which are familiar to many managers, despite the fact that the theories are difficult to apply. Both theories are 'universalist' because they assume few differences between individuals. We have included these theories, however, so that when you hear other managers speak of 'hygiene factors' you know what they mean.

Activity 2

Allow 3–4 hours for this activity.

There is a choice in this activity. Option 1 is to analyse and plan to resolve an individual's current motivation problem. This option is easier to carry out than the second option and may provide immediate benefits to performance. However, you may not be able to identify a suitable individual or you may find that, after starting with what you believed to be a suitable individual, the problem disappears or is found to be too difficult to make useful progress. If so, choose Option 2, which asks you to plan what you will do differently as a result of your learning this week when motivating others in the future. This second option does not focus on an individual.

Background to Option 1

You can choose someone whose motivation is generally too low or too high or someone who is suitably motivated for some parts of their work, but not others. You can choose one or several individuals. Here are some suggestions.

- Individual A: a member of your work group or project group. This is likely to work well if there is a satisfactory or positive communication climate between you.
- Individual B: you. Choosing yourself might work well if you feel you have a motivation problem but have been too busy to investigate it carefully. A possible difficulty with this choice is that you might find that you are spending too much time on the activity. Another possible difficulty is that your investigation might lead to negative emotions which would be inconvenient at this time.
- Individual C: a colleague. You could focus on a problem that a colleague is having, provided he or she is willing to provide the time you will need to investigate the issue fully.

Further guidance

If you choose Individual A, a member of your work group or project group, make sure that the problem or area for improvement is one over which you can exercise influence. It is very easy to construct a long list of what your organisation could do, but is not likely to do, to improve the individual's motivation. This does not really help you manage the individual better. As people are not necessarily motivated by the same things, make sure that the focus of the activity is an individual rather than a group.

To carry out the activity, you will need to:

- think back over what the individual has said, done and not done which might be evidence of their motivation

- have some discussion(s) with the person concerned, so you should allow time for this. Note that the need for discussion means it is not possible to consider a past motivation issue.

We strongly recommend that you do not choose an individual who is undergoing or might undergo an organisational procedure such as 'performance improvement' or a disciplinary procedure. Note that your organisation's formal procedures may not allow you to collect information for a motivation activity.

The way you approach your evidence collection will link to how open or closed you see the communication climate. The success of your discussion will be influenced by the communication climate between you and your work group generally, and particularly between you and the individual you have chosen. Chapter 2 included a reading on the communication climate.

You will need to consider how the person might react to your request for a discussion unless you are carrying out this work as part of your day-to-day management role. If you are not, we strongly recommend that you explain that the discussion is part of your activities for your management studies and that the individual can choose not to participate. Make clear what will happen to the information you collect. You need to be ready for questions such as: 'If I give you private and personal information, what will you do with it?' and 'How will the information I provide be used in future annual performance appraisals, promotions?'

Background to Option 2

If you select this option then your response to Activity 2 will be rather different. However, it will still contain an analysis of your current practices and some 'solutions' – how you will change them and why. Potentially, this second option is more difficult than the first one because it will require you to look at your practices, interpersonal skills and communication (and the communication climate you create). In proposing changes to your practices, you will need to consider the way in which you can increase your understanding of those you manage and what motivates them. Thus, your response to the activity will not be focussed on any one individual but will be a general approach or set of practices that will help you to understand and maintain the motivation of those you manage.

Option 1

Identify a situation where a person's motivation is generally too low or too high or where someone is suitably motivated for some parts of their work, but not others. Analyse the situation, draw conclusions and plan a solution that will solve or improve the current situation and prevent it recurring.

Use Table 7.1 to help you structure your problem-solving. Questions to guide you and advisory notes are included.

Table 7.1 A motivation problem

Problem identification and description	What is the issue or problem? To whom is it a problem and why? What are the symptoms of the problem or issue? What is their impact?
Analysis	Using the motivation theories set out in the readings, what do you think are the main causes? What are the views of the person concerned? What assumptions have you made? Are there any gaps in your analysis?
Conclusions to the analysis	What is your overview? (Include the important causes of the problem and significant features of your analysis)
Recommendations	What would you like your solution to achieve (criteria)? How might you resolve the problem? Consider various options and discuss these with the person concerned. You may decide on more than one possible solution and this is acceptable. For example, you may need to find how your line manager or HR manager responds to alternative solutions. Note that some motivational problems disappear when they are discussed, without further intervention. This would be the case if a person felt demotivated because they felt ignored (you are now doing the opposite of that) or if, during discussion, they realised that they had an unrealistic expectation of the manager, or of the organisation. These are useful learning points, so even if the problem disappears, record them and consider what you might do to prevent the same motivational issues recurring. If there is a problem to solve, decide whether and what intervention might be necessary. These may be changes to the way you manage the person (or how the colleague or you are managed) or changes that need to be agreed with more senior managers. These changes may concern changing or adjusting management practices. It is also possible that you will find there is no solution to the problem – or none that is in your power to bring about (for example, a change in the nature of a person's job). If there is a possible solution, set out a set of recommendations that are SMART.

Table 7.1 continued

	Ensure that you recognise any organisational constraints in your criteria for a solution and recommendations. Use module concepts and themes. Ethics may be relevant: have you developed a solution that is fair to other people in the work group? State any assumptions that you have had to make.
Advantages, disadvantages and implications	Consider advantages and disadvantages of your solution. How feasible is your solution? Consider its implications. What wider changes for the organisation (for example, in systems/communication) have your recommendations suggested? Say how you might deal with important disadvantages and reduce the impact of particular implications, if this is possible.

The content of this activity would not normally be the subject of a report unless systemic changes were needed in the organisation.

Option 2

Plan what you will do differently as a result of your learning this week from now on when working with others. Use Table 7.2 to structure your response. Statements and questions are provided to help you. It would be useful to discuss some of your new ideas with members of your work group in a general way, while you are carrying out the activity. For example, you could ask them what they expect of the organisation and whether they feel they are sufficiently rewarded in various ways for their efforts; what changes in practice (yours and the organisation's) they would like. However, there is a danger of creating unrealistic expectations of change, if the changes required are beyond your control.

Table 7.2 What I will do differently

How I currently note and deal with changes in the level of motivation of those I manage	Your current methods may be a mix of formal and informal ones. Identify the most important ones (which may be informal). When people feel demotivated or upset, who initiates a discussion – or is there little discussion? It would be useful to look back to the monitoring methods in the control loop in Chapter 4.
What I learned from my reading on motivation	

Table 7.2 continued

Proposed changes to my practice	Consider your current practices and how you might change them, or incorporate opportunities for discussion. Justify these changes – say how the change will improve staff motivation. Also consider what associated changes you might need to make. These might be physical changes such as a notice board or more comfortable chairs in the meeting room. Do you need to improve your communication skills, or improve the communication climate in your work group? Are there other problems, such as lack of cohesion and trust, within the work group, or a problem with the way in which performance is appraised? Although you have not studied some areas of the module relevant to these issues, note them now. They can form the basis of a problem-solving activity later in the module. What are the advantages, disadvantages and implications of the proposed changes to your own practices?
What requires changes that are beyond my own control and what I will do about it	Now consider here where your current practices, or possible changes to them, cannot resolve an issue. You may well be able to create a more open communication climate that benefits the work group. You could ensure that you praise efforts and take more interest in how work group members feel about their work, and learn what motivates them and what particular individuals are working towards. You can also adjust your own expectations of your staff. However, you will have little influence over organisational expectations. Identify these, consider and justify what might be done.
Implementation plan for proposed changes	Develop a set of criteria for changes in organisational expectations – what a revised set of expectations should achieve. Then consider what you might propose to more senior managers. Make all your proposals meet your criteria and that they are SMART!
Advantages, disadvantages and implications	Consider the advantages, disadvantages and implications of the changes you might propose to more senior managers.

While carrying out this activity, you may have identified a general motivation issue that you were not previously aware of. Or you may have found that, in your organisation, systems and practices are such that motivation is generally high, and any demotivation is quickly identified and addressed. In this case, you may have found little room for improvement. However, you will have increased your awareness of your own practices, and in doing so taken a step towards more effective management.

Activity 2 output

- *A completed version of Table 7.1 or Table 7.2.*

This week's activities and readings should have provided you with an opportunity to gain insight into what influences the types of job people may choose to do and their relationship with their job and with the organisation they work for. While motivation theories are difficult to apply, you can use key aspects of them as the basis of discussion with individual staff so that you can identify and address motivation issues before they have an impact on performance and on others in the work group.

Week 7 activity outputs

1 A summary of your responses to questions.

2 A contribution to the Week 7 activity forum containing all or part of the summary.

3 Three key points on the similarities and differences between your own (selected) beliefs, values and motivations to work and at work and those of at least two other students.

4 A completed version of Table 7.1 or Table 7.2.

Learning outcomes

After completing this set of activities and readings you should be able to:

- recognise the importance of understanding personal difference in managing professional relationships
- understand motivational theories and how you can use them as a practising manager
- know how to identify and address a motivation problem at work
- understand how your own day-to-day management practices can have an impact on motivation.

Week 8 Understanding leadership

Introduction

Many factors including people's personal beliefs and expectations play a part in their performance at work. However, the behaviour and skills of managers and leaders will also have an influence in guiding people to work towards their own and the organisation's objectives. This week, we look at managers' ability to lead. We ask the question: 'What is leadership?' and consider different views on who leaders are and what they do. Then we focus on how you can develop your own leadership skills and capabilities. Coaching and mentoring are considered as possibilities for leadership development. The main activities for this week will be to identify a leadership skill you need to develop and plan how to develop it.

Week 8 Activities

- Activity 1 Consider and discuss your own experiences of leaders, leading and being led. (Allow 1 hour for this activity.)
- Activity 2 Analyse the types of leadership skills needed in your own organisational context. (Allow 1 hour for this activity.)
- Activity 3 Identify a leadership skill you need to work on and plan how you could address it. (Allow 3 hours for this activity.)

Week 8 Readings

These readings are in *Managing and managing people*, Chapter 7, 'Understanding leadership' and Chapter 11 'Learning and development at work'.

- Reading 1 Leadership in practice (Chapter 7)
- Reading 2 Leadership in context (Chapter 7)
- Reading 3 Developing leadership skills (Chapter 7)
- Reading 4 Coaching and work-based learning and development (Chapter 11)
- Reading 5 Mentoring and personal and professional development (Chapter 11)

Activity 1

Allow 1 hour for this activity.

Anyone who has worked in an organisation will have had experience of being led – that is, of being influenced in various ways to achieve organisational goals and perhaps personal ones. You are likely to have a variety of experiences to draw on, good or poor, allowing you to make comparisons. The first part of this activity asks you to draw on these experiences to explore what you think good leadership is and what it means to you. In the second part of the activity, you will share your views with other students.

First, consider the people who have influenced you, or currently influence you. What skills do these leaders have that enabled them to influence you? What behaviours have you noted? What has been the effect of these skills and behaviours in influencing – or even inspiring – you to perform well and work effectively towards goals? These leaders will have shaped the way you define leadership and the understanding you now have of it. So this activity is designed to help you consider your current understanding of leadership – and how you exercise leadership in your work as a manager now. Use Table 8.1 for this activity. You can include leaders from outside work because these people are likely to have influenced your understanding of leadership as much as leaders in the organisations in which you have worked. Note that the people you choose to describe do not have to be in formal leadership roles. When completing Table 8.1, describe each leader in terms of their role and your role at the time. In some cases you may need to describe the relationship if the person who influenced you was (or is) a colleague or a friend.

Table 8.1 Examples of leaders, skills, behaviour and impact

Description of leader	Examples of their leadership	Skills and behaviours exhibited	Effect on me

When you have completed Table 8.1, post your completed version of it to the Week 8 activity forum. If necessary, first remove any indentifying information from your completed table. Read other students' contributions. Have they chosen very different examples of leadership? Have they identified very different or similar skills and behaviours? Were the effects similar or different? Draw some conclusions from your comparison in about 150 words. Do any differences you found mean that leadership means different things to different people or that leadership can take a variety of forms? Or does it mean both of these – that some types of leadership appeal to some people more than others and that different types of leadership can depend on the context in which people lead? Do similarities mean that there may be some core leadership skills and behaviours? Post your conclusions to the Week 8 activity forum and read other students' conclusions.

This activity will have prompted you to think about what you think leadership is or means to you. The people you described may be different in terms of background, experience and gender but each will have guided or led you using particular skills and behaviour in a particular context. The first part of the activity was likely to have been the simplest part, however. In the second part you probably found that your fellow students did not identify the same leadership skills and behaviours that you wrote down. It should not surprise you if, after you posted your conclusions, debate in the activity forum was lively: leadership is exceptionally hard to define!

Activity 1 outputs

- *A completed version of Table 8.1.*
- *A contribution to the Week 8 activity forum containing a completed version of Table 8.1.*
- *A contribution to the Week 8 activity forum containing your conclusions on similarities and differences.*

Readings 1, 2 and 3

The first reading, *Leadership in practice*, in Chapter 7 addresses some of the difficulties in describing what leadership is and includes some attempts to define it. Some traditional approaches to the study of leadership are also examined – trait theories, style theories and contingency theories.

The second reading, *Leadership in context*, in Chapter 7 focusses specifically on the implications of leadership for managers. It considers the role of leadership in twenty-first century organisations and the concept of leadership as a process – that different people play different roles at different times to influence people in acceptable ways. As you read, consider the implications of this idea for managers, and for your own role.

Then read *Developing leadership skills*, in Chapter 7, which covers specific leadership skills by dividing leadership into different categories of task and the skills and behaviours required for each. Make a note of the tasks in which you are involved, and the skills and behaviours you need or need to develop. This will help you with Activity 2.

As you work your way through the readings, you might reflect on Activity 1. How similar are the ideas you put forward to those in the texts? You may also wonder where management skills 'end' and leadership skills 'begin'. There is considerable overlap: managers are invariably leaders, at least some of the time in some situations. However, not all leaders are managers. Consider your own work group members. Do any demonstrate leadership in particular circumstances? What do they do, or how do they do this?

Activity 2

Allow 1 hour for this activity.

This activity helps you to analyse leadership – your own and that of other people – in your own organisational context and to identify some of the influencing skills required.

Use the frameworks you have just read about in Reading 3, *Developing leadership skills*, to identify the leadership tasks you and the people around you perform on a day-to-day basis in your jobs and the influencing activities and skills you and they use. Use Table 8.2 for your output. To complete it, consider the behaviours listed by Yukl (2004) in Reading 3.

Choose some behaviours that are relevant or significant in your work context (but select no more than two or three from each category). Give an example of each of these chosen behaviours. Then indicate who performs them. It may be you, or someone more senior (or more junior). Finally, indicate how you or the person you have identified influences others. Select from the forms of influence in the second part of Reading 3, but do not be reluctant to include other forms of influence; the reading does not provide a complete list, only the most common ones.

Table 8.2 Leadership behaviours and influencing skills

	Examples*	**Who leads or influences**	**Influencing skills used**
Task behaviours			
Relations behaviours			
Change behaviours			

*Add rows as necessary.

This activity should have helped you to identify how some aspects of leadership are 'done' in your organisation, your department or group. You may have chosen leaders/influences at various levels in the organisation; certainly, you will have chosen those who are visibly influential. What about your own leadership behaviours and influencing skills? When comparing ourselves and our skills with more experienced others, we can often see where there is room for improvement!

Activity 2 output

- *A completed version of Table 8.2.*

Readings 4 and 5

These two readings are in Chapter 11. *Coaching and work-based learning and development* and *Mentoring and personal and professional development* are of general relevance in professional development. They are useful at this point in the module, however, because of their particular value in developing leadership skills. Many skills such as those required for leadership can be learned but cannot be taught in the usual ways. Thus, other methods must be found. In coaching and mentoring, a person who is more experienced helps a less-experienced person either by focussing on specific knowledge, skills and tasks (coaching) or on general personal and professional development (mentoring). The differences between coaching and mentoring are made clear in the readings, together with advantages and disadvantages of each approach. As you read, consider how you might use one or other approach to enhance any leadership skills that you would like to improve. Why might you choose a coach and not a mentor (or a mentor rather than a coach)? What would you want from coaching or mentoring? What roles would you want a coach or mentor to play? What roles would you definitely not want a coach or mentor to play? How will you go about finding a coach or mentor? Make notes to help you with Activity 3.

Activity 3

Allow 3 hours for this activity.

In this activity you are asked to identify and analyse a current or recent work situation in which your leadership is or was not fully successful because one or more of your leadership skills was insufficient. Then you will work out a solution to developing this skill/these skills which may involve coaching or mentoring (formal or informal). You do not have to include coaching or mentoring as part of your solution, however. The activity assumes that you do not already have a coach or mentor. If you do, you can still choose coaching or mentoring as the means by which you can improve a skill or develop your leadership capabilities. Follow the guidance provided in Table 8.3.

Try not to choose a situation in which issues other than leadership were the causes of difficulty. For example, even good leadership skills may not be sufficient to avoid difficulties when there are insufficient staff to achieve a goal, or when a project's objectives are changed by senior management due to unforeseen circumstances. If you cannot identify a work situation, then identify a suitable one outside work in one of your other roles – for example, sports club secretary.

Use Table 8.3 to structure your activity output. It contains questions to guide you, many from the GROW model from Reading 4 *Coaching and work-based learning and development*. Note that, under the heading Recommendations, in addition to developing criteria for a solution you are asked to develop options before selecting one or more options and setting out SMART recommendations.

Table 8.3 Improving leadership skills

Problem identification and description	What is/was the situation and the issue or problem? To whom is or was it a problem and why? Are or were there any other impacts?
Analysis	What are/were the 'symptoms' of this problem? Are/were there different aspects to it? How do these relate to your leaderships skills? Which leadership skill(s) in particular? Do you have any evidence that a lack of such skill(s) caused these particular symptoms? What assumptions is it necessary to make?

Table 8.3 continued

	Are there any gaps in your analysis? Are module themes, such as ethics, relevant? Use relevant module concepts, tools and techniques and diagrams to aid your analysis.
Conclusions to the analysis	What is your conclusion? Try to step back and develop an overview. What particular leadership skills do you need to develop and why, based on your analysis?
Recommendations	1 Set out criteria for a solution What are your long-term and short-term goals? When do you want to achieve them? Are there any organisational constraints that you need to consider? 2 Develop options, using relevant module concepts How much control do you have over your goals? What available options for development are there? Are there any that are currently not available in your organisation that you could ask to be made available? Are there informal options that might achieve the same purpose? 3 Consider the options Which options best meet your needs? What are the advantages and disadvantages of these options? Which would you be reluctant to use and why? Which appeals most? Whose support do you need? If you choose coaching or mentoring, what do you need to consider? Who might you choose and why? If you already have a coach or mentor, consider whether the person is likely to be able to help you. If not, why not? Does the person have the expertise? Does the relationship require renegotiating? 4 Select one or more options (if more than one solution needs to be put in place) and set it or them out as a set of SMART recommendations.

Table 8.3 continued

	State any assumptions you have had to make. If you have chosen coaching or mentoring as a solution, then you will also need to include a SMART plan for identifying a possible coach or mentor, seeking their agreement, and a first discussion on needs and expectations. Use relevant module concepts and themes in your recommendations.
Advantages, disadvantages and implications	Consider these carefully. You will have already identified advantages and disadvantages of the options you developed so, here, you will need only to set out the advantages and disadvantages of the options you selected. However, you may find it useful to refer to ethics when setting out advantages. You may not have considered implications earlier. If you chose mentoring as a solution, for example, what would be the implication of the mentoring relationship being unsuccessful? Have you taken account of the situation in which your leadership skills appeared insufficient: how will the people you are leading or trying to influence be likely to react to any change in your behaviour? Will they welcome and support it? This, perhaps, best underlines the guidance provided earlier: be sure to choose a situation in which leaderships skills are or were the main cause of difficulty. Say how any disadvantages or negative implications might be mitigated.

You are not required to write up your completed version of Table 8.3 in report format, unless you wish to do so for your own purposes. If you do, it will be helpful to refer back to the format and guidance provided for Week 4, Activity 4 to ensure that you include the appropriate information in each part of the report.

This problem-solving activity may have been one of the most difficult you have undertaken in the module so far. It can often be quite easy – if rather uncomfortable – to recognise a lack of professional skill in ourselves. It can be far more difficult to work out a remedy, and more difficult still to implement it. Sometimes, having considered the options, we realise that we have too little time, or that there are insufficient resources, or that we do not feel very enthusiastic about spending time and effort just now, while studying and coping with commitments outside work. However, it can be surprising how differently we can feel about something when we receive support – from our line manager, colleagues, friends and family – and when the organisation we work for actively supports our professional development, providing opportunities at work and in work time. Later in the module, when we look at how managers can develop other people, it will be useful to reflect on the activity you have just completed.

Activity 3 output

- *A completed version of Table 8.3.*

Week 8 activity outputs

1 A completed version of Table 8.1.

2 A contribution to the Week 8 activity forum containing a completed version of Table 8.1.

3 A contribution to the Week 8 activity forum containing your conclusions on similarities and differences.

4 A completed version of Table 8.2.

5 A completed version of Table 8.3.

Learning outcomes

After completing this set of activities and readings you should be able to:

- understand why leadership is necessary in organisations
- understand the context of leadership and its different forms
- understand the difference between management and leadership
- identify leadership behaviours and skills and when they are needed
- understand the purpose and use of coaching and mentoring to improve leadership skills.

Week 9 Working in groups and teams

Introduction

Being able to work with people so that the right things happen is a core management skill. Managing people effectively perhaps demands most of managers when individuals come together to work in a group or in a team, which requires leadership as well as facilitating and overseeing group and team working, and managing conflict. This week we explore team working from start to finish. This includes deciding if the creation of a group or team is the best approach to the task in hand (it is not always!), selecting individuals to work in it, setting up the team-working processes, supporting teams through the different stages of development, reviewing progress and evaluating team outputs. The main activity involves problem-solving, based on a current situation with a team or group that you manage or with which you are familiar.

Week 9 Activities

- Activity 1 Reflect on your own experience of working with others in a group or team. (Allow 20 minutes for this activity.)
- Activity 2 Summarise your group or team experiences, based on your learning from readings. (Allow 40 minutes for this activity.)
- Activity 3 Evaluate or review a group's or team's effectiveness using tools provided in the readings. (Allow 1 hour for this activity.)
- Activity 4 Identify, analyse and plan to resolve a current problem in a team or group you manage or are familiar with. (Allow 3 hours for this activity.)

Week 9 Readings

All readings are in *Managing and managing people*, Chapter 8 'Working in groups and teams'.

- Reading 1 Making teams work: an introduction
- Reading 2 Creating successful teams – a holistic view
- Reading 3 Team roles
- Reading 4 The life cycle of a team
- Reading 5 Managing team processes
- Reading 6 Managing conflict
- Reading 7 Reviewing and evaluating team performance
- Reading 8 Modern forms of groups and teams (optional)

Activity 1

Allow 20 minutes for this activity.

This activity is designed to help you to consider the range of issues that managers need to be aware of in order to understand and successfully manage group and team work. This will help to prepare you for the readings that follow, which take a holistic approach to the team-work process.

First, consider a team or group in which you have participated. You can choose a work group or team, or a group or team from another area of your life, for example, a voluntary action group or team.

Now respond to the questions in Table 9.1. Note any other thoughts not prompted by the questions. Your responses may help you in Activity 2.

Table 9.1 Group/team work: a reflection

What was the purpose of the group or team?
How well did it achieve its goals and aims?
Who was involved in it?
How were members selected?
Did they have different skills and experiences?
If so, were they complementary?
What processes and activities worked well and what did not work so well?
What are the positive features you can remember?
What are the negative features you can remember?
Other thoughts

This activity was probably not too difficult if the group or team you chose was, for example, a work-based project team. In these cases, it is sometimes difficult to know when to call a group a team. In long-serving groups and teams, goals and objectives can also change over time. In voluntary groups, members may select themselves. Sometimes it is hard to judge the extent of difference between the skills or experiences that members have if the group or team is short-lived, or if members are required to carry out a very similar task without very much interaction. Thus, you may have found some questions were not as easy to answer as they seemed at first.

Activity 1 output

- *A completed version of Table 9.1.*

Readings 1 and 2

Now read *Making teams work: an introduction* and *Creating successful teams – a holistic view*, both in Chapter 8.

The first reading provides a general introduction to groups and teams used in workplaces, when they are needed, and how the task influences the size and constitution of a group or team. In many organisations groups are referred to as teams, but there are differences which you should be able to identify as you read. The second reading focusses on an 'open systems' approach' to teamwork – a helpful approach which encourages managers to consider the context in which a team works. The approach considers team processes, which are divided into three parts: *inputs*, *throughputs* and *outputs*. These highlight the different issues and activities a manager needs to engage with or oversee during the life of a team. To prepare for Activity 2, read with a specific team in mind. It could be the team you referred to in Activity 1 or a different one. Ideally it should be a workplace group or team that you manage (or one in which you participate or have participated). Think about the processes the team went through (or will go through). Make notes as you read.

Activity 2

Allow 40 minutes for this activity.

Using the notes you made, complete Table 9.2 covering the inputs, throughputs and outputs (actual or anticipated) of your group or team. (You do not have to use the group or team you used in Activity 1.) The group or team should be one that you manage or in which you participate or which you managed or participated in during the recent past. Use the input, throughput and outputs questions in the reading *Creating successful teams – a holistic view* to help you. You should be able to answer these questions, or make informed judgements, even if the group or team has not completed its task (or it is a permanent one).

The first purpose of this activity is to help you to consolidate your thinking to help you draw on past experience to inform present and future practice. The second purpose of the activity is for you to assess whether groups or teams operate in more or less the same way in organisations. To do this, post your table to the Week 9 activity forum. Read the contributions of at least two other students and compare and contrast them with your own. Then write three key points on the similarities and differences you found. There is no template for this: use a Word file for your three key points.

Table 9.2 Inputs, throughputs and outputs

Purpose of group or team
Inputs
Throughputs
Outputs
Particular success factors
Improvements that could have been made

(Source: based on Schermerhorn et al., 1995 in Ingram et al., 1997)

In carrying out these activities you probably found the questions in the text invaluable; however, you may have thought of other good and relevant questions.

Activity 2 outputs

- *A completed version of Table 9.2.*
- *A contribution to the Week 9 activity forum containing a copy of Table 9.2.*
- *Three key points on similarities and differences, based on a comparison of your own summary with those of at least two other students.*

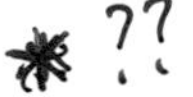

Readings 3 to 7

These readings set out in more detail some of the inputs, throughputs and outputs, how to manage throughputs and how to review team progress and evaluate its performance when the task is complete. Reading 3, *Team roles*, in Chapter 8 needs to be treated with caution. Teams are often put together on the basis of the availability and skills of individuals, and managers are often not in a position to select team members. Yet such teams can and do function well. However, Belbin's theory of team roles is popular and influential so it is important that you know about it. What managers really require is an understanding of how people are likely to behave in a team. But note that the behaviour of people is not fixed: it is influenced by context and the behaviour of others.

Reading 4, *The life cycle of a team*, in Chapter 8 covers the stages that teams normally go through, from forming to disbanding. Note that the stages cannot always be clearly identified: this is likely to be the case if a team operates for a few days or if a team has changes in its membership. In the first case, there may be little 'storming' and in the latter there may be a considerable amount of it.

Reading 5, *Managing team processes*, in Chapter 8 covers mainly throughputs and some advice on management. As you study Readings 3 to 5, consider what you might do to make a difference to the management of a group or team you are responsible for, or what you might do differently with a future team.

Reading 6, *Managing conflict*, in Chapter 8 is one that is generally applicable to the management of people, not just groups and teams. You are likely to refer back to it in future weeks of the module. It will help you to identify sources of conflict and the ways in which conflict can be managed. Note that not all conflict is bad: sometimes it can be constructive, if handled effectively. There are times when it is better to ignore conflict. However, in each case, you will have to use your judgement.

Reading 7, *Reviewing and evaluating team performance*, in Chapter 8 sets out a number of approaches a manager or team leader can use for ongoing review and final evaluation. Readings 3, 4 and 5 inform the content of the checklists and questionnaires presented in Reading 7. You will need to select one or more approaches for Activity 3, so it would be a good idea to assess their usefulness as you read.

Activity 3

Allow 1 hour for this activity.

Use one or more of the tools or techniques in Reading 7, *Reviewing and evaluating team performance*, to review or evaluate a group or team you currently manage or participate in to assess its effectiveness. If necessary use a team you recently managed or participated in. The technique of observation is often very useful but cannot be carried out if the group or team is no longer operating. If you want to observe a current group or team, it will take more preparation and time than using the other tools and techniques. Observation needs the consent of all members of the group or team. Thus, you are advised not to choose this technique without consulting your team and your tutor, who will provide specific advice. All of the techniques are best used in conjunction with team members because the views of group or team members may differ (and be different from your own). People can feel threatened when performance and effectiveness are reviewed. This is more likely if it happens irregularly and if they are not involved in the process. For this reason, you may want to answer the questions based on your own experience and views. You will have to do this if you do not lead or manage a group or team or if it is too difficult to get consent from the manager/leader and members for such a discussion.

Choose one or more tools and techniques and respond to the questions, issues or statements in the selected tools or techniques. Identify the tools and techniques you have used and record your responses in Table 9.3. Add more rows as necessary, according to the tool or techniques you have chosen.

Table 9.3 Reviewing/evaluating performance

Technique or tool used:
Question, issue or statement 1:
Response:
Question, issue or statement 2*:
Response:

* Add rows as necessary.

This activity is likely to have revealed issues that you perhaps had not considered while reading. It should help you to identify an issue or area for improvement to work on in the final activity this week.

Activity 3 output

- *Identify the tools and techniques you have used and record your response in about 200 words.*

Reading 8 (optional)

You will need to read this if the group or team you want to focus on in the final activity is a virtual or multicultural group or team. Reading 8, *Modern forms of groups and teams*, in Chapter 8 covers the particular needs created when the primary means of communication is via ICT and when there is cultural diversity.

Activity 4

Allow 3 hours for this activity.

Your task in Activity 4 is to identify a current group or team problem or area for improvement, analyse it and set out your recommendations for addressing it. If the team is one you lead or manage, you may be able to implement your proposed solution immediately, thus improving the effectiveness of the group or team. If you are basing the activity on a group or team you led or participated in during the recent past, then your proposed solution should enable you to consider how you might revise your group and team work and management practices.

Your work on Activities 2 and 3 should have helped you to identify a number of potential problems or areas for improvement. Select what you consider to be the most important. This is likely to be something that has the greatest impact on team effectiveness, such as conflict in the group or team.

Use the questions in Table 9.4 to guide you through the activity and the table headings as a template for your response. If you find that you cannot resolve the problem for some reason, say how it might have been avoided. Note that under recommendations, in addition to setting our criteria for a solution, you are asked to develop options to choose from before setting out your SMART recommendations.

Table 9.4 Group or team issue

Problem identification and brief description	What is the issue or the problem? To whom is it a problem and why? Are there any other impacts?
Analysis	What are the 'symptoms' of this problem? What are the different aspects to it? How do these relate to team inputs, throughputs and outputs? What information do you have to hand about the issue? What extra information do you need? Who do you need to talk to? Then, assuming you are able to acquire sufficient information, analyse the causes of the problem. Use module concepts, tools and techniques and diagrams to help you. If you discover limitations in the concepts you use, then say what they are – identifying them will help you analyse the problem more fully. Are there any gaps in your analysis? What assumptions do you need to make? Use module concepts, tools and techniques, and customised diagrams to help you with your analysis. Module themes may be relevant to particular aspects of it.

Table 9.4 continued

Conclusions to the analysis	What do you conclude? Try to achieve an overview and set out important causes of the problem and significant features of your analysis.
Recommendations	What are the criteria for an effective solution – what do you want your solution to achieve? Recognise organisational constraints both in your criteria and when developing options. What are the options for addressing the issue or problem and what are they? Note here that your choices are likely to depend on the degree of influence you have, but do not restrict yourself too much: you may be in a position to influence others. How could these options address the problem or areas for improvement that you identified? How well does each meet your criteria for a solution? Which option appeals to you most and why? Which would you be reluctant to use and why? Who else do you need to work with or influence? Select one or more options (if more than one solution needs to be put in place) and set it or them out as a set of SMART recommendations. State any assumptions you have had to make. Say how you will monitor, review or evaluate the success of the solution(s). Use relevant module concepts and themes.
Advantages, disadvantages and implications	Consider these carefully. When working with groups and teams, implementing solutions can sometimes be complex if all group or team members need to be involved. Implications can mean that a solution is unworkable if it requires, for example, additional resourcing which you are unable to secure. Set out how particular disadvantages or negative implications might be addressed, making sure that any plans are SMART. Refer to module themes if they are relevant.

Unless the problem you identified was relatively small, internal to the group and did not involve an input problem, such as a mismatch between the group or team and task, then you are likely to have found it more difficult to identify a solution than to identify the problem. Indeed, it may be the case that a solution seemed impossible and you may have resorted to how the problem might have been avoided. Although you will have no solution to implement, you will be able to draw lessons to inform your current and future management practices.

We have not made writing a report a compulsory part of Activity 4. If you intend to use the activity in Part 1 of TMA 02 you will need to write up your response in report format in about 750 words either now or later. It will be helpful to refer to the guidance provided in Week 4 Activity 4 to ensure that you include the appropriate information in each part of the report.

Activity 4 output

- *A completed version of Table 9.4.*

Week 9 activity outputs

1 A completed version of Table 9.1.

2 A completed version of Table 9.2.

3 A contribution to the Week 9 activity forum.

4 Three key points on similarities and differences, based on a comparison of your own summary with those of at least two other students.

5 A completed version of Table 9.3.

6 A completed version of Table 9.4.

Learning outcomes

After completing this set of activities and readings you should be able to:

- recognise the difference between groups and teams and understand when each is more appropriate
- understand issues in team constitution (team roles)
- identify the different stages of team development and how a manager can support the team at each stage
- understand and identify team processes (inputs, throughputs and outputs) and the manager's role
- understand and manage conflict
- review and evaluate the performance and effectiveness of groups and teams
- identify and plan how to resolve a problem concerning a group or team.

Week 10 Recruiting and selecting staff (1)

Introduction

As a manager your job is likely to include managing people. You are likely to spend time monitoring the performance of staff and providing or arranging training and development to improve their skills. But first you have to recruit suitable staff. When you have recruited people who do not do their jobs well – or the manager before you has – it creates many problems. One might be a person who does not fit into the team. Another might be a person who is so unsuccessful in their job that you need to remove them from their role. In most circumstances it is far better and less costly to recruit the 'right' people into a role and into the organisation in the first place. Over the next two weeks we explain how that might be done. This week we focus on the requirements of a role; next week we focus on how you might recruit to fill that role.

Each week there is a choice of activities. Choose the Option A activities if you are unfamiliar with recruiting and selecting staff. Choose Option B activities if you already involved in recruiting and selecting staff. Do not sometimes choose an Option A activity and sometimes an Option B activity: the output of some activities become the input to a later activity, in particular the Option A activities. Option A activities involve planning while some Option B activities offer opportunities to investigate and make suggestions to improve unsatisfactory current situations or to learn lessons from them if it is too late to make changes to them.

However, we know that some of you work in organisations in which recruitment and selection processes are of high quality and where areas for improvement are hard to find. Option A activities, while they may not use exactly the same processes as those used in your organisation, will familiarise you with the fundamental techniques and processes used in recruitment and selection. You can then compare these with how recruitment and selection is carried out in your organisation, if you wish to extend your learning. Option B activities offer you choices depending on the quality of the processes in your organisation. Do not be concerned if you are not in a position to change how things are done in your organisation. This is often the case in a larger organisation in which recruitment and selection is managed by an HR department. However, you may still be able to influence processes.

We suggest that you read the activity options for Weeks 10 and 11 before making your choice of Option A or B activities. Make sure you have work situations that you can use in the Option B activities. The activities are listed below in a fuller form than usual.

Week 10 Activities

Activity 1

Option A

- Write a job description for a familiar role, locate the actual job description if one exists and compare your description with the existing job description or that of the role-holder. (Allow 2 hours for this activity.)

Option B

- Prepare a job description for a role that does not have one, or has changed or is unsatisfactory in some way. If your organisation has high-quality recruitment and selection processes you may need to choose a work role in a different organisation, for example, a previous job you had, or that of a friend or family member. (Allow 2 hours for this activity.)

Activity 2

Options A and B

- Find out about the anti-discrimination and diversity guidance or policy in your organisation as it applies to recruitment and selection.

Or

- If there is no guidance or policy, find out about the anti-discrimination laws that apply to recruitment and selection in your country.

Or

- If your organisation regularly reminds you of its guidance, policies and processes, look again at the current documents.

Whichever of the alternatives you choose, then do the following.

Consider why sometimes managers do not comply with these requirements. Also consider how these requirements influence your current behaviour in recruitment and selection or will do so in future when you are involved in recruitment and selection. Share your thoughts with other students in the Week 10 activity forum and summarise organisational differences. (Allow 90 minutes for this activity.)

Activity 3

Option A

- Write a person specification based on the job description you created in Activity 1 and which complies with anti-discrimination policy or laws. (Allow 90 minutes for this activity.)

Option B

- Write a person specification for the job description that you produced in Activity 1 for a changed or problematic role. Ensure that the person specification complies with anti-discrimination policy or laws and assess the extent to which the role holder fits the new person specification. (Allow 90 minutes for this activity.)

Or

- Review and attempt to improve on a person specification, based on an existing job description and person specification. Ensure that the existing or amended person specification complies with anti-discrimination policy or laws and assess the extent to which the current role holder fits the existing or amended person specification. State whether or not you were able to make changes to the existing person specification, what they were and how they improved the person specification. (Allow 90 minutes for this activity.)

Either alternative is suitable if your organisation has high-quality recruitment and selection processes. The second one will provide insight into quality processes.

Week 10 Readings

All readings are in *Managing and managing people*, Chapter 9 'Recruiting and selecting staff'.

- Reading 1 The importance of managing recruitment and selection well
- Reading 2 Job analysis and the creation of a job description
- Reading 3 Person specification

Readings 1 and 2

Reading 1, *The importance of managing recruitment and selection well*, in Chapter 9 covers exactly what is meant by recruitment and selection and why managing the process well is usually important. Unless you have experience of involvement in all the stages previously, you may be surprised by the complexity of the process and how the outcomes of each stage must be the basis for the next. Note, however, the importance of considering not just the job that needs doing but the organisation the new staff member will work for. How do the two concepts of person–job fit and person–organisation fit match your own experience of new people joining an organisation?

Reading 2, *Job analysis and the creation of a job description*, in Chapter 9 sets out what job analysis is and ways of approaching it. Note that there is scope here for redesigning a job. This may be necessary if an existing job has changed or needs to be changed. An example would be when an organisation must manage with fewer staff. However, the focus of the text is an existing job. From the job analysis, a job description is created. Recall when you last applied for a job: how important was the job description to you in being able to assess whether it was the job you wanted? Looking back, how accurate was it?

Activity 1

Allow up to 2 hours for this activity.

Option A

In this activity you will create a job description for a role with which you are familiar and compare your description with the formal description (if one exists). It is preferable, therefore, to choose a role for which a job description exists, although this is not essential. You are advised to choose your own role or a recent role you performed. If this is not possible, or if you are so familiar with your job description that you would not learn much from the activity, then choose the role of someone you work with. You should be sufficiently familiar with the role to be able to identify the key responsibilities without consulting the formal job description (if there is one) and without discussion with the role holder unless you are prepared to spend more time on the activity. Contact your tutor if you have any difficulty in selecting a role.

When you have chosen the role, if possible find or ask for the actual job description for the role, but do not read it. Then write a job description without consulting the actual description. In writing the job description you might find it useful to consult the list of questions suggested for a job analysis (Reading 2). If you are describing the role of someone other than yourself, and find it necessary to clarify some aspects of the job with the person, you will need to allow time for this. Make it clear to them that you are carrying out a learning activity as part of your management studies. You may also need to ask the person for their formal job description. Using your notes, write the job description.

Use Table 10.1 to structure your description. An example of how you might complete the activity and what your output might look like is given in Box 10.1. Table 10.2 shows the questions used to obtain information and Table 10.3 sets out a job description.

Table 10.1 Job description

Post title
Location and department
Reports to
Summary of role
Specific responsibilities

Box 10.1 A job description for Brian

Jane is the Call Centre Manager at Bradford's Bank. She wanted a job description for the role of Senior Call Centre Handler in her team. To create the job description, she asked Brian, the most experienced Senior Call Centre Handler in her team, about his role. Jane's questions were the same as those used in job analysis in Reading 2. She wrote down Brian's responses in Table 10.2.

Table 10.2 Brian's responses

Question	Brian's answer
What do you do in your role?	My role is to answer telephone queries from existing customers and to find out answers to their questions (usually about their account). I am also required to try to sell the bank's other products. Some queries can be received by email or letter. I must ensure that all enquiries are logged on the bank's customer relation database.
When do you do what you do?	I am contracted to work 35 hours a week in the call centre and this work can be at any time between 8.00 a.m. and 8.00 p.m. Monday to Saturday (the call centre's opening hours). Each week a rota is put up and I then know what my shifts will be. The agreement with the bank is that each call handler will work only one Saturday out of four.
Where is the work done?	I work in the call centre in Manchester, a city in the north-west of England. The call centre covers this region of the country. From time to time I am required by the Call Centre Manager to visit another call centre for a meeting.
How is the work done?	I answer each query in the time limits set down and ensure that the customer is aware of the option of talking to a sales adviser about the products on offer. I must also deal with the query as far as I can. Sometimes, this means I need to ask a colleague for the information, although it is my responsibility to ensure that the customer receives the correct answer to their enquiry. When answering queries I must follow a basic script. I am expected to answer an average number of queries each day and to generate three new opportunities or leads a day for a sales person to call the customers with a view to selling them a new product.
Who do you report to?	The Call Centre Manager
Are you responsible for managing anyone and if so who?	I don't have responsibility for managing anyone but as part of my role from time to time I am asked to mentor a new recruit to the call centre. This means that I will train them in some aspects of the role and will be available for questions.

Table 10.2 continued

Who do you communicate with, what do you communicate, and how?	The key people I communicate with are customers. I also need to communicate with other members of the team (when asking questions) and sales advisers (when passing them a lead). From time to time I receive calls from customers outside this region and it is my responsibility to transfer these calls to the appropriate regional call centre.
Do you have any responsibility for planning and organising and if so of what or whom?	Part of Senior Call Handler role involves reviewing the weekly rota once the Call Centre Manager has created it and checking there are no problems with it.
Do you provide any general administrative support and if so what?	Most queries are dealt with over the phone but some need to be followed-up by letter or email. It is my job to ensure that this happens.
Does your role involve any monitoring and reporting and if so of what and to whom?	No
Does your role involve any evaluating and decision-making and if so what?	No
Does your role involve any financial budgeting and control and if so of what?	No
Are you responsible for producing, creating or developing anything and if so what and how much?	No
Do you have responsibility for maintaining or repairing things and if so what?	No
Do you have any responsibility for quality control?	Yes, as part of my role I am asked to listen to calls taken by junior call handlers. I check that the calls are being answered using the script and that the junior call handlers are dealing with customers appropriately. Once I have listened to the calls I report back to the Call Centre Manager.
Are there any health and safety considerations in your job?	None outside those normally required for staff.
Are you required to use equipment and systems?	Yes, I need to be able to operate a computer and use a number of the bank's electronic systems as well as to be able to use the call centre's telephone system.
Is there a requirement for self-development in your job and if so, in what area?	Yes, I am expected to remain up-to-date with the bank's main processes and procedures.

Table 10.2 continued

Are there any other responsibilities that arise that do not fit within your general role?	Yes, from time to time the Call Centre Manager will ask me to produce a report for her and she has indicated that she may have other requirements on occasions.

From this information Jane was able to summarise Brian's role. Her summary is set out in Table 10.3.

Table 10.3 Jane's job description for a Senior Call Centre Handler

Post title	Senior Call Centre Handler
Location and department	Manchester Call Centre (with occasional travel to other locations)
Reports to	Call Centre Manager
Summary of role	To answer queries from customers using call centre guidelines and procedures and to ensure that customers receive accurate and full answers to their queries. To ensure that customers contacting the bank are aware of the range of services that may be of value to them. To provide other support to the Call Centre Manager as required.
Specific responsibilities	To work as the weekly rota requires. To answer telephone calls, emails and letters coming in to the call centre from customers in a timely manner and using call centre procedures. Following an enquiry, to ensure that the appropriate systems are updated both with details of the call and any changes to the customers' circumstances. To ensure that any enquiries that are not dealt with immediately are followed up in a timely manner. To make customers aware of other products and services that may be of value to them. To pass on any enquiries for further information to an appropriate sales adviser. To maintain an up-to-date knowledge of the bank's policies, practices and procedures as they relate to customers. When requested by the Call Centre Manager to provide new members of staff with training, support and guidance. On behalf of the Call Centre Manager to review the weekly rota prior to publication to identify any potential issues. From time to time to attend meetings on behalf of the Call Centre Manager. To make regular checks on the quality of telephone calls taken by other call handlers and to provide feedback to the Call Centre Manager. To undertake other work from time to time as requested by the Call Centre Manager.

We hope you found the example in Table 10.3 useful. If you followed it you will have avoided going into too much unnecessary detail: writing a job description requires you to stand back and be objective. If you chose your own role as the basis of your job description, you may have found this difficult!

When you have written your version of the job description compare your list of responsibilities with those in the formal job description for the role you chose, if a formal description exists. If it does, in about 100 words, write three reasons why you think these differences exist. (There is no template for this, so create a Word file.) You may find that the formal job has undergone significant change, although the job description was accurate when you started. For example, there may have been an increase in responsibilities or the introduction of new systems may have changed how you do your work. Alternatively the actual job description may never have accurately reflected the true nature of the role. You may want to find out more about how the job description was first constructed. If there is no existing job description or if you are unable to obtain it, you will not be able to carry out this part of the activity. Instead, note down in a Word file three learning points from the activity in about 100 words.

Activity 1 Option A outputs

- *A completed version of Table 10.1.*
- *Three reasons for differences between the formal job description and your own*

Or

- *if a formal job description does not exist, three learning points from the activity.*

Option B

In this activity you will create a job description for a role that doesn't have one, or for a role that has changed since the original job specification was written or is unsatisfactory in some way. If it is not possible to identify a changed or unsatisfactory role in your organisation or your part of it because the organisation has high-quality recruitment and selection processes, you can prepare a job description for a work role in a different organisation, for example, a previous job you had, or that of a friend or family member.

The lack of a job description, or changes in the role, are likely to have led to difficulties, such as:

- lack of role clarity
- aspects of the original role are no longer being performed
- the role-holder is trying to carry out too many tasks and the performance of some is affected
- a person is carrying out tasks for which they are not qualified.

Ideally, the role-holder will be a person you are responsible for but you may have to choose a role-holder in a different organisation who is experiencing or has experienced one or more of the difficulties set out above. Whatever the case, be prepared to explore the person's role with them. In the case of a work-group member, make it clear to the person that you are carrying out a learning activity as part of your management studies unless you are conducting the task as part of your professional work. Note that the module activity does not include the implications of amending a job description: radical changes to an existing job description, if there is one, are likely to result in changes in contractual arrangements. Further, if the role becomes vacant in the future, time will need to be spent amending the job specification, or creating one.

Read the contents of Box 10.1 to guide you through the creation of a job description. Use Table 10.1 to structure your job description. By following it you will avoid going into too much unnecessary detail. The format of the job description (and processes) provided in Box 10.1 and Table 10.1 may differ from those used in your own organisation. You can use the format and processes we have set out, or those that your organisation uses. If you use your organisation's versions, compare the formats and processes and note the advantages and disadvantages of each. This will extend the time you spend on this activity but it will provide you with insights into the formats and processes your organisation uses. If they are of high quality you will see why they are; if they need improvement you will see where and why.

Finally, consider and then describe in about 150 words *one* of the following:

- if no previous job description existed, the situation you identified and what you discovered from creating a job description

Or

- if a previous job description existed, the key differences between the existing one and the one you created

Or

- if you used a different job description format and processes from those set out above, the key advantages and disadvantages of each.

There is no template for this part of the activity: create a separate Word file.

You may have found that the role you chose to consider has undergone significant change, for example, there may have been an increase in responsibilities or the introduction of new systems may have changed what the person does. Alternatively, the original job description, if there was one, may never have accurately reflected the nature of the role, or the role-holder may have expanded or reduced the role without consultation. You will have identified the reason for lack of role clarity or problems in the performance of the role and you may now be in a position to make improvements. Alternatively, you may have been able to provide valuable insights to help a friend or family member.

Activity 1 Option B outputs

- *A completed version of Table 10.1.*
- *Notes describing how the creation of a job description helped you to understand the situation you identified, including a brief description of the situation*

Or

- *if a previous job description existed, the key differences between this previous job description and the one you created*

Or

- *the key advantages and disadvantages of the formats and processes used here and those used in your organisation.*

Reading 3

Now read *Person specification* in Chapter 9. Pay particular attention to the UK Office of National Statistics example provided. While you are reading, consider how a recruitment process could be biased.

Activity 2

Allow 90 minutes for this activity.

Options A and B

Are you aware of your organisation's policy on anti-discrimination? Most large organisations have policies or guidance that relate to recruitment and selection. These policies may go beyond what anti-discrimination laws require. For example, they may celebrate the diversity among staff and typical job advertisements may say that the organisation welcomes applications from people from different ethnic groups. Smaller organisations may have informal policies or no policies at all but simply comply with anti-discrimination laws. Yet others may not comply with some or all of these laws.

In this activity you are required to find and understand the formal anti-discrimination and diversity guidance or policy of your own organisation, or country laws that apply to recruitment and selection. In multinational organisations where the laws of several countries apply to recruitment and selection in different parts of the organisation you will need the guidance or policy or laws that apply to the country you are working in. Guidance and policy documents or information are normally available from your Human Resources or Personnel department. Many students who work in an organisation with neither of these will know who to ask. If after a search you can find no-one who can tell you the organisation's policies, then consult your tutor.

Alternatively, you may not have to carry out any research at all. In some organisations, staff automatically receive policy updates on diversity and discrimination. If this happens in your case, remind yourself of your organisation's policy on diversity and discrimination and any recent updates.

However, if there is no guidance or policy, find out about the anti-discrimination laws that apply in your country. In many countries this information is available on government websites and others that provide guidance on recruitment and selection. If you have difficulty finding the information you need, other students in your tutor group or in the Student Café may be able to provide guidance. It is helpful here for all students to share information freely about possible sources of information in different countries. However, your tutor will be able to help if are not able to find the information you need.

Your tutor may ask to see the guidance or policy so copy and save the information you find or retain paper copies. In the case of country laws, save copies of relevant web pages. Then carry out the following steps.

Step 1 Indicate in Table 10.4 whether organisational guidance and policy exits or not.

Step 2 Consider the key points of the guidance, policy or laws and indicate in Table 10.4 what you are allowed or not allowed to discriminate against. If discrimination is allowed in some circumstances, note down these and briefly set out the reasons.

Some examples of situations that involve discrimination, and which may be permissible, include:

- religious organisations might not be able to recruit people into key positions unless they have the same religious beliefs
- in the health and care sector, gender discrimination may be necessary in some areas for roles involving particular types of personal care
- in some areas of social welfare, people from ethnic minorities and who speak particular languages may be sought for some roles
- a country may require organisations to employ a specified proportion of people with that country's nationality by a particulate date.

If you are using guidance or policy supplied by your organisation, the circumstances in which discrimination may be allowed and reasons why are often stated. If not, then make some informed judgements or ask Human Resource or Personnel staff.

If you are using country laws, you do not need to cover all the circumstances in which discrimination might be permitted. Consider only your own organisation, or the part of it with which you are most familiar.

Whether you are using guidance or policy documents provided by your organisation, or country laws, you do not have to provide detailed and comprehensive information, only the most important and obvious circumstances and reasons for any discrimination in your organisation or your part of it.

Step 3 Consider whether you and the managers in the parts of your organisation you know well follow the guidance, policy or laws enthusiastically, sufficiently, or not at all. Consider, too, why this is so.

In the case of diversity, an organisation may value and pursue it because this supports the forward-looking and inclusive reputation is has created and seeks to maintain, or because of the candidates that particular roles attract. Another organisation may claim to value diversity, but this is not reflected in the staff selected. Yet another organisation may be silent on diversity and comply only with anti-discrimination laws.

While some forms of discrimination may be permitted in particular circumstances, discrimination can also occur for other reasons. For example, it may just seem inappropriate for a middle-aged woman to join a young, all-male IT team. In other cases discrimination may result from the specific prejudices of more senior staff. You may work for an organisation in which managers actively tell you to appoint or to avoid appointing people from a particular ethnic group, or gender. You may have prejudices too! For example, you may believe that people of a particular nation or who have particular religious beliefs are morally superior or inferior. Such prejudices can be embarrassing to admit to. They can also be hard to recognise and to overcome if others around you share similar prejudices.

When you have assessed the extent to which managers in your organisation, or your part of it, comply with guidance, policy or country laws on discrimination, complete the appropriate part of Table 10.4. Also consider why in some cases there may be a mismatch between policy (or laws) and behaviour of these managers (including, perhaps, your own). Note down the reasons in the table.

Step 4 Now assess how the guidance, policy or laws influence your behaviour or will influence it in the future when you are involved in recruitment and selection. Summarise your thoughts in the appropriate part of Table 10.4.

Step 5 Share your still-incomplete Table 10.4 with other students in the Week 10 activity forum. Check first that you have been as factual as you can be. You may not want to share some information, for example, any personal prejudices you have, but you should be aware of them and of the way in which negative generalisations can limit thinking and action.

Step 6 Read the postings of at least two other students, seeking any clarification that you need, and then summarise similarities and differences between guidance, policies or laws and practices in the three organisations (one of which will be your own). Write your summary in the last part of Table 10.4.

The information you have collected will be useful when you carry out Activity 3 (Options A and B).

Table 10.4 Discrimination and diversity

1. Does guidance/policy exist in the organisation?	Yes, on discrimination and diversity Yes, on discrimination only No, country laws only
2. Discrimination is not allowed/is allowed against:	
Gender	Yes/No If yes, for what reasons in the organisation you work for?
Disability	Yes/No If yes, for what reasons in the organisation you work for?
Ethnicity (nationality, race, colour)	Yes/No If yes, for what reasons in the organisation you work for?
Beliefs (religious, political)	Yes/No If yes, for what reasons in the organisation you work for?
Age	Yes/No If yes, for what reasons in the organisation you work for?
Class/caste or family background	Yes/No If yes, for what reasons in the organisation you work for?
Dress/personal appearance/particular clothing such as head covering (turban, burqa or purdah)	Yes/No If yes, for what reasons in the organisation you work for?
Criminal record	Yes/No If yes, for what reasons in the organisation you work for?
Other (specify), e.g. new recruits must have relatives working in the organisation or in the same profession	Yes/No If yes, for what reasons in the organisation you work for?
3. Extent to which guidance/policy/laws are or are not followed in a familiar part of the organisation and why	
4. How the guidance/policy/laws influence or will influence my behaviour	
5. Summary of similarities and differences between guidance/policy/laws and practices in three organisations including my own	

Some parts of this activity are likely to have been uncomfortable to carry out. However, if you (and your fellow students) were honest about any differences between policy (or laws) and practice and the difficulties of avoiding some forms of discrimination, then you are likely to have gained insight into some ethical dilemmas. You may need to consider such dilemmas next week. Consider, for example, the example of an elderly man in a wheelchair with a passion for fashion applying to be a sales assistant in a boutique selling clothes for young women. In some countries the man could claim he was being discriminated against on grounds of gender and age and perhaps disability if he were the best-qualified candidate for the job but was not offered it. In recruitment and selection we may carefully target our advertising to avoid such situations, but we may be confronted nonetheless with many, more-subtle situations. The final part of the activity – reading about and comparing policies and practices in other organisations – may have provided reassurance. Compliance with guidance, policies and laws is seldom straightforward, even when people do not act on their personal prejudices or those of more senior managers.

Activity 2 outputs

Options A and B

- *A contribution to the Week 10 activity forum containing a version of Table 10.4 with relevant parts completed to allow a comparison of organisational policies (or country laws) and practices.*
- *A completed version of Table 10.4.*

Activity 3

Allow 90 minutes for this activity.

Option A

Now you are ready to take the next step. After developing and writing a job description, you now need to produce a person specification that accurately reflects the ideal person for the job. Write the person specification for the role you selected in Activity 1 for the creation of a job description. Consider carefully what qualifications, work experience, knowledge, skills and physical abilities will be required for a person to do the job successfully. Also consider any organisational requirements, for example, a particular set of values or attitudes.

In creating the person specification, avoid referring to any existing person specification. Also make sure that it complies with your organisation's policy on diversity and discrimination, which will normally conform to any state legislation in place.

Use Table 10.5 to create your person specification. Add rows as necessary to the writable version of it. Column 1 provides a guide to the categories of criteria you will want to include but you may want to add a category. In column 2, describe each criterion in the category and the level required. You may want to list each criterion in a separate row. In column 3, indicate whether the criterion *must* be met by candidates or whether it is desirable but not essential. How to measure skills and knowledge (column 4) is covered next week but, in the meantime, consider whether some skills and knowledge are best tested by some way other than simply by talking to a person during an interview. As part of the activity you are asked to verify that your person specification complies with your organisation policy (formal or informal) on diversity and discrimination (or country laws).

Table 10.5 Person specification Option A

Job title:			
Organisation:			
Criteria (categories)	***Description of criteria in each category including level***	***Essential/ desirable***	***Measured by***
Qualifications			
Work experience			
Knowledge			
Skills			
Organisational requirements			
This person specification complies with organisational policy on diversity and discrimination (or country laws).Yes/no			

It may have been quite easy to identify the skills, knowledge and experience required for the role you chose, but less so to work out which skills, knowledge and experience were essential and the level required. You may also have given considerable thought to whether listing too many things as essential might result in too few applicants, and whether listing a particular level or type of experience as essential might contravene your organisation's discrimination policy (or country laws). If you based your person specification on your own job, you may have inadvertently focussed on your own skills rather than on those that fitted the job description you created. It can be hard to assess what qualities are essential for a person to do the job effectively, because the job may not necessarily be done exactly the way it is done now.

Activity 3 Option A output

- *The current version of Table 10.5 (Table 10.5 needs to be completed next week).*

Option B

This activity involves writing or reviewing a person specification. You can either:

- Write a person specification for the job description of the changed or problematic role. You can base this person specification on the job description you produced in Activity 1.

Or

- Review and attempt to improve on a person specification. To do this you will need a copy of the original job description and the person specification.

Either alternative is suitable if your organisation has high-quality recruitment and selection processes. The first one allows you to focus on a role in a different organisation, as you may have done for Activity 1. If you chose this alternative it will provide an opportunity to continue to understand how to improve the quality of recruitment and selection. The second alternative will provide insight into quality processes. Whichever alternative you choose, you will need to ensure that the new or reviewed person specification complies with anti-discrimination policy or laws. You are also asked to assess the extent to which the role holder fits the new person specification. If you are reviewing a person specification you are asked in addition to indicate any changes, why and how they improved the person specification.

In each case you will have a job description to work from and your intention is to write or improve a person description so that it is more appropriate or fit-for-purpose. You might want to introduce some criteria for 'person–organisation fit', for example, or specify personal skills. Or you might want to reconsider or reduce or increase the number of essential skills because you encountered or expect to encounter difficulties in finding suitable candidates (either too few or too many).

First, consider the job description carefully and decide what qualifications, work experience, knowledge and skills will be required for a person to do the job successfully. Also consider any organisational requirements, for example, a particular set of values or attitudes. If you are reviewing an existing person specification, consider what you would change.

Use Table 10.6 for your output. Add rows as necessary to the writable version of it. If you are reviewing an existing person description some or all of the information will be the same as the existing person specification in the first four columns.

Column 1 provides a guide to the categories of criteria you will want to include but you may want to add a category. In column 2, describe each criterion in the category. You may want to list each in a separate cell. In column 3, indicate whether the criterion *must* be met by candidates or whether it is desirable but not essential.

Leave column 4 blank for the moment. How to measure skills and knowledge is covered next week but, in the meantime, consider whether some skills and knowledge are best tested by some way other than simply by talking to a person during an interview.

In column 5, note any differences (so far) between the original person specification and the new one, why you made these changes and how they improve the person specification. Do this if you are reviewing and trying to improve on an existing person specification. If you are creating a new person specification you will be able to complete this column only if you have access to the original person specification. This may not be available.

Make sure that the new or amended person description complies with your organisation's policy on diversity and discrimination, or country laws. An organisation's policy will normally conform to these. If you are basing your person specification on the job description of a friend or family member working in an organisation other than your own, you can use the guidance or policy of the organisation the person works for if it is easy to obtain, or country laws. Now verify that your person specification complies with the organisation policy on diversity and discrimination or country laws.

Table 10.6 Person specification Option B

Job title:				
Organisation:				
Criteria (categories)	***Description of criteria in each category including level***	***Essential/ desirable***	***Measured by***	***Differences between existing and amended person specification, why changes were made and how they improve the existing one***
Qualifications				
Work experience				
Knowledge				
Skills				
Organisational requirements				
This person specification complies with organisational policy on diversity and discrimination (or country laws): Yes/no				

Reviewing, rewriting or writing a person specification is likely to have been satisfying and useful for planning improvements to a current or future recruitment and selection exercise (or helpful to a friend or family member while providing practise for you). It may have been quite easy to identify the skills, knowledge and experience required for the role you chose, but it was probably more difficult to work out which were essential and the level required. You may also have given considerable thought to whether listing too many things as essential might result in too few applicants, and whether listing a particular level or type of experience as essential might contravene your organisation's discrimination policy.

If you were trying to improve on an existing person specification, perhaps you were unable to make as many improvements to it as you had hoped to make: if so, column 5 of Table 10.6 may have very few entries so far. It will be valuable to consider why this is so. In many larger organisations, this task is carried out by specialists in an HR department, and their work may be difficult to improve on without the necessary training and experience. That is not to say that person specifications in smaller organisations are always in need of improvement, but where recruitment and selection is carried out fairly infrequently there is unlikely to be the same level of expertise.

Activity 3 Option B output

- *The current version of Table 10.6 (Table 10.6 needs to be completed next week).*

Week 10 activity outputs

Option A outputs

1 A completed version of Table 10.1.

2 Three reasons for differences between the formal job description and your own OR if a formal job description does not exist, three learning points from the activity.

3 A contribution to the Week 10 activity forum containing a version of Table 10.4 with relevant parts completed to allow a comparison of organisational policies (or country laws) and practices.

4 A completed version of Table 10.4

5 The current version of Table 10.5 (Table 10.5 needs to be completed next week).

Option B outputs

1 A completed version of Table 10.1.

2 Notes recording how the creation of a job description helped you to understand the situation you identified, including a brief description of the situation

Or

if a previous job description existed, the key differences between this previous job description and the one you created or amended

Or

the key advantages and disadvantages of the formats and processes used here and those used in your organisation.

3 A contribution to the Week 10 activity forum containing a version of Table 10.4 with relevant parts completed to allow a comparison of organisational policies (or country laws) and practices.

4 A completed version of Table 10.4.

5 The current version of Table 10.6 (Table 10.6 needs to be completed next week).

Learning outcomes

After completing this set of activities and readings you should be able to:

- understand appropriate recruitment and selection processes and why they are important
- assess the need to recruit
- produce or review and revise a job description
- produce or review and revise a person specification
- be aware of and understand how to apply organisational policy on discrimination and diversity.

Week 11 Recruiting and selecting staff (2)

Introduction

So far we have covered the first steps in the recruitment and selection process – analysing a role, creating or recreating a job description and then a person specification which accurately describes the skills, experience and abilities the job holder should possess. Now we consider how to attract a good selection of candidates and to ensure that your selection processes allow you to distinguish between candidates and find the most appropriate one. This is a challenge for even the most experienced of managers! A further issue that we cover is the cost of recruitment – and the cost of getting it wrong.

There is a choice of activities. Choose the Option A activities if you are unfamiliar with recruiting and selecting staff and you chose the Option A activities last week. Choose Option B activities if you are already involved in recruiting and selecting staff and you chose Option B activities last week. Do not sometimes choose an Option A activity and sometimes an Option B activity: the output of some activities become the input of a later activity, in particular the Option A activities.

The main Option A activity this week is to plan the selection for a vacancy. This is a continuation of last week's activities when you prepared a job description and person specification. Your recruitment and selection plan will be based on this. In Option B the main activity is to identify and investigate an unsatisfactory recruitment and selection process in order to learn lessons for next time. If you work in an organisation in which recruitment and selection processes are of high quality and you are not able to identify any unsatisfactory processes, then base the activity on the recruitment and selection processes used when you were recruited for a previous job or on the recruitment and selection of a friend or family member who works in a different organisation from your own. Alternatively, you can continue with your review of processes in your own organisation.

Week 11 Activities

Activity 1

- Option A Prepare a recruitment and selection plan. (Allow 3 hours for this activity.)
- Option B Investigate and revise an unsatisfactory recruitment and selection plan

Or

- review a recruitment and selection plan. Compare your plan with the original one. (Allow 3 hours for this activity.)

Activity 2

- Options A and B Assess the recruitment and selection plan using the 4Es, invite comments on the plan and provide feedback on a plan developed by another student. (Allow 1 hour for this activity.)

Activity 3

- Option A Compare your recruitment and selection plan with recruitment and selection practice in your own organisation. (Allow 30 minutes for this activity.)
- Option B Draw conclusions from your comparison of your recruitment and selection plan with the original one in order to gain insight into why recruitment practice can be a key factor in retention of staff. (Allow 30 minutes for this activity.)

Week 11 Readings

All readings are in *Managing and managing people*, Chapter 9 Recruiting and selecting staff.

- Reading 1 Marketing the job vacancy
- Reading 2 Shortlisting job applicants
- Reading 3 Selecting applicants
- Reading 4 Designing and conducting a selection interview
- Reading 5 Ethics in recruitment and selection
- Reading 6 Induction and socialisation

Readings 1, 2, 3 and 4

These readings lead you step-by-step from attracting applicants through shortlisting and the different selection methods to how to design and conduct an interview (the most common selection method). You may want to carry out Activity 1 in stages as you study the readings. Alternatively, make notes that you can use for Activity 1, which we suggest you read now to familiarise yourself with it.

Reading 1, *Marketing the job vacancy*, in Chapter 9 considers some of the methods for attracting applicants to a role. As you read this, think about some of the limitations associated with each of the methods. Questions to ask include: What types of applicant are likely to be attracted by each method? Which of these methods is best suited to the job description and person specification you created last week?

Then read Reading 2, *Shortlisting job applicants*, in Chapter 9. This provides guidance on how to shortlist your candidates after applications have been received. This reading includes an example of the shortlisting of candidates for a role. You might find it useful to consider why each of four candidates has been shortlisted. This section also explores some of the limitations of application forms and CV data. Applicants often exaggerate their claims. Does this match your own experience?

There are many different methods of choosing between candidates for a job. Reading 3, *Selecting applicants*, in Chapter 9 explores the most commonly-used methods and some of their advantages and disadvantages. You may have experienced some of them personally. As you read consider the methods most likely to be suitable for the role you described last week and the person specification you created or revised. In particular, look at the *essential and desirable criteria* in your person specification. Are there any selection methods that you might now add to the 'Measured by' column? How would you, personally, feel about being assessed by the methods you choose? Do you think that, together, they are sufficiently fair?

Although an interview may be only part of a selection process, it is commonly-used but often poorly planned and carried out. Reading 4, *Designing and conducting a selection interview*, in Chapter 9 sets out how to plan and conduct interviews. Pay particular attention to the types of question used, and how they help interviewers find out the information they need. As part of Activity 1 you will need to write a basic set of questions if your selection plan includes an interview.

Activity 1

Allow 3 hours for this activity.

Option A

In this activity you will plan the recruitment process for the job description and person specification that you created in Week 10. The texts you have just read should have provided some guidance on good practice. However, you may find that there are constraints on using some of the marketing or selection methods that seem most attractive. For example, using a recruitment agency may seem to be a good idea because it will reduce your workload. However, this may be too expensive for the level or nature of the role. Your plan needs to achieve its aim and also meet the constraints set by the organisation.

Your plan should include:

- How each of the essential and desirable criteria in the person specification will be measured during the selection process.
- How you will market the job, with a justification of your choices.
- How you will select applicants, again justifying your choice of selection methods.

Step 1 First complete the final column of Table 10.5, the person specification you created last week. Try to select the simplest methods, while ensuring that the selection is appropriate and sufficiently fair. For example, you can check any necessary or desirable qualifications by asking candidates to bring certificates when they attend for selection. You may choose to check their skills by devising a work sample test.

Step 2 Now select, describe and justify methods of advertising this role, and set out the advantages and disadvantages of each method chosen. Use the appropriate section of Table 11.1 for this. Add extra rows as necessary to the writable version of the table. When justifying your choices it will not be sufficient to say that 'national newspaper' advertising will target a wider audience. You will need to name the publications you have in mind (in the description column). You also need to justify these choices in terms of how they will reach the target audience; for example, some newspapers may be known for advertisements for particular types or categories of jobs. You will need to do the same for websites too. If you are unsure, your HR department or colleagues may have a good knowledge of which publications and websites are best for particular types of jobs. Interestingly, they may not use some publications or websites (or some other methods of advertising) that produce many requests for application forms or details but result in very few applications being made. Targeting your advertising is quite an art.

Marketing is an area in which you are likely to encounter organisational constraints. These are likely to be caused by existing processes or cost issues. They may prevent or dissuade you from using one or more methods. Consider the advantages and disadvantages of each method and assess particular advantages against organisational constraints in your own organisation.

If you are focussing on your own or another job in your own organisation, you may also want to approach your HR department to see whether there is a standard approach for marketing the type of job on which you are focussing. It is likely that you will have to conform to this. You are not confined to the methods set out in Reading 1, *Marketing the job vacancy*, in Chapter 9 but, if you choose other methods, be sure to provide some details about them.

Step 3 Identify, describe and justify the selection methods you will use to choose between candidates. You will need to provide a short description of how each selection method will work; for example, for a work sample you will need a brief outline of its design. If you are intending to include an interview, say whether or not this will be a panel interview in the 'Description' column, together with the types of questioning to be used. Also set out the list of questions you will need to ask to cover the intended areas. You should also set out the advantages and disadvantages of each method you choose. The advantages and disadvantages you list should be based on the job on which you are focussing and not on the general benefits or shortcomings of the method.

Use the appropriate section of Table 11.1 to structure your output to this part of the activity. You are not confined to the methods set out in Reading 3, *Selecting applicants*, in Chapter 9 but, if you choose other methods, be sure to describe them well. Include what they are designed to test and how they will be used.

Table 11.1 Marketing the job and methods of selection

Job title:			
Organisation:			
Marketing			
Method	***Description***	***Justification***	***Advantages and disadvantages in this case***
Method 1			
Method 2			
Method 3*			
Selection			
Method*	***Description/detail***	***Justification***	***Advantages and disadvantages of method for this job***
Interview(s)	Description of interview type List of basic interview questions		
Work sample(s)	Outline of design		
Personality tests			
Aptitude tests	What aptitudes are to be tested		
Assessment centre	Description of test mix		

* Add rows as necessary

** Delete methods you have not selected.

If you have not been involved in recruitment and selection before, this activity is likely to have highlighted the planning and decision-making that the process needs. When you were reading, you may have wondered why many job advertisements are placed in local or national newspapers (including newspapers with job vacancy websites). You may also have wondered why interviews are the most common method of selection when so many others are available and may be more effective. Now you may realise why these choices are so popular! Alternatively, you may have been creative in your thinking and considered several ways of reaching a target audience and some simple, effective selection methods.

Activity 1 Option A outputs

- *A completed version of Table 10.5.*
- *A version of Table 11.1 (the table will be amended in Activity 2).*

Option B

For this activity you have several choices. Choose *one* of the following.

1. Review a current or recent recruitment and selection exercise that was unsatisfactory in some way and then compare your plan with the original

one. Identify a situation in which you suspect, or know, that advertising was poor, or that the shortlisting and selection was faulty. It may be that the original job description or person specification was poor, and, when these were attended to – perhaps in last week's Option B activities – advertising and selection also needed to be changed. In the case of a recent recruitment and selection exercise, you may not be able to rectify the situation but you are likely to be able to take some lessons forward for next time.

2. If you work in an organisation in which recruitment and selection processes are of high quality and you cannot identify a recruitment and selection exercise that was unsatisfactory in any way, choose an unsatisfactory example outside the organisation such as that of a friend or family member. Prepare a new plan and then compare your plan with the original one.

3. Alternatively, you can write a recruitment and selection plan based on person specification you reviewed in last week in Activity 3. Then compare your plan with the original one.

Whichever of these Option B variants you select, together with the final one this week, you will have an opportunity to see how to improve the process of attracting and choosing staff, or in the case of variant 3, to gain further insights into quality practices.

IMPORTANT NOTE

Whichever variation of the activity you choose, you will need a person specification. This can be the one you created or reviewed last week in Activity 3, or an existing one if you have selected a different case to work on. The first step is to locate (or ask for) the person specification for the post – or the one you created or reviewed last week. You will also need the original recruitment and selection plan or sufficient information about it to make a comparison later. For variant 3 of Option B, it is best to have the actual recruitment and selection plan.

The instructions for the activity differ slightly if you are using a person-description you have not created or reviewed. These are set out in Box 11.1 *Using an existing person specification.*

Your plan needs to achieve its aim and also meet the constraints set by the organisation.

Your plan should include:

- How each of the essential and desirable criteria in the person specification will be measured during the selection process.
- How you will market the job, with a justification of your choices.
- How you will select applicants, again justifying your choice of selection methods.

Step 1 First complete the final column of Table 10.6, indicating how you will measure each selection criterion.

Box 11.1 Using an existing person specification

If you have chosen to work on a new case and have not created or reviewed the person-specification for the role, you will not be able to complete the final column of Table 10.6. The contents of the table will relate to a different role. Instead, complete the first column of Table 11.2 under Selection methods. Using the information in the person specification you have, consider how each selection criterion could be measured most effectively and efficiently. If selection methods have been listed in any information that accompanied the person-specification, assess how effective these methods might be and identify improvements if necessary. Note down in Table 11.2 what methods *you* would use.

Then note down in the last column of your version of Table 10.6 that this is incomplete because you are working on a new case. You will not be penalised for an incomplete table if you use it as part of your assessed work.

Try to select the simplest methods of measurement, while ensuring that the selection is appropriate and sufficiently fair. For example, you can check any necessary or desirable qualifications by asking candidates to bring certificates when they attend for selection. You may choose to check their skills by devising a work sample test.

Step 2 In column 1 of Table 11.2 in the section *Marketing the job* list the methods you have decided are most appropriate and in column 2 describe them briefly. In column 3 justify methods of advertising this role that you think are more appropriate, again setting out any advantages or disadvantages. Make sure that the advantages and disadvantages of each method are specific to the use of the method for the job, rather than general advantages and disadvantages of the method. There are almost certain to be some disadvantages! Add extra rows as necessary to the writable version of Table 11.2. Some further guidance is set out below.

When justifying your choice of methods it will not be sufficient to say that 'national newspaper' advertising will target a wider audience. You will need to name the publications you have in mind (in the description column) and to justify these choices in terms of how they will reach the target audience; for example, some newspapers may have a reputation for carrying advertisements for particular types or categories of jobs. Perhaps lack of attention to such factors in the original recruitment and selection plan lead to problems of this sort. You will need to name and justify choices of website too. Try not to use publications or websites (or some other methods of advertising) that produce many requests for application forms or details but result in very few applications being made.

In your consideration of the advantages and disadvantages of each method, assess their particular advantages against the organisational constraints in your own organisation or the one in which the role-holder works. This is particularly important if you are introducing methods that are not used or seldom used in the organisation. These constraints may be financial or existing processes. There may be a standard approach for marketing the type of job on which you are focussing; however, this may be why the current or recent marketing and selection process is or was unsatisfactory. You are not confined to the methods set out in Reading 1, *Marketing the job vacancy*, in Chapter 9 but, if you choose other methods, be sure to provide some details about them.

Step 3 Identify appropriate selection methods, describe them and justify their use in the *Selection methods* part of Table 11.2. Further guidance is set out below.

To help you to complete the *Selection methods* part of Table 11.2, refer to the person specification you created or the existing one. Consider the ways the essential and desirable criteria are to be measured: these will help you to select appropriate selection methods. For each method you choose you will need to provide a short description of how it will work; for example, for a work sample you will need an outline of its design. If an interview is one of the selection methods you have chosen, say whether or not it will be a panel interview in the 'Description/detail' column, together with the types of questioning to be used. Also set out the list of questions you will need to ask to cover the intended areas. Then justify the methods you have chosen and be clear about the advantages and disadvantages of each method.

You are not confined to the selection methods set out in Reading 3, *Selecting applicants*, in Chapter 9 but, if you choose other methods, be sure to describe them well. Include what they are designed to test and how they will be used.

Step 4 Now refer to the original recruitment and selection plan, or seek sufficient information to allow you to compare it with the plan you have just created. Complete the remaining columns of Table 11.2 using the original plan or information about it. Unless you have a copy of the original plan, in some cases you may not have a complete description and details of the selection methods, for example, the list of interview questions. You should be able to work out what they were from the person who was interviewed, however, and what questions might not have been asked. Finally, consider the advantages and disadvantages of your own plan over the original one and list them.

This activity is likely to have highlighted the planning and decision-making that went wrong in an unsatisfactory recruitment and selection process and what can be done better next time. The next recruitment and exercise you are involved in may not be for the same role, especially if you based the activity on the recruitment and selection of a person in another organisation, but the systematic thinking you did will help you when you are next involved in recruitment and selection. If the recruitment and selection exercise is a current one occurring in your work group or your part of the organisation, it may not be too late to make changes to improve the process. If so, the activity will have been particularly satisfactory. If you were continuing your review of recruitment and selection processes in your own organisation, you will know why the processes are of high quality – or you may have found room for improvement. If this is the case, then you may feel confident enough to make suggestions next time you are involved in recruitment and selection.

Table 11.2 Marketing the job and methods of selection

Job title:						
Organisation:						
Marketing						
Methods	**Description**	**Justification including advantages and disadvantages**	**Original methods**	**Description**	**Advantages and disadvantages of new or adapted marketing plan over original one**	
Method 1			Method 1			
Method 2			Method 2			
Method 3*			Method 3*			

Selection

Essential/desirable criteria (for use if a new case has been chosen)	**Method****	**Description/ detail**	**Justification including advantages and disadvantages**	**Original method**	**Description/detail of original method**	**Advantages and disadvantages of new or adapted selection plan over original one**
	Interview(s) • Description of interview type • List of basic interview questions			Interview(s) • Description of interview type • List of basic interview questions used		
	Work sample(s) • Outline of design			Work sample(s) • Outline of design used		
	Personality tests			Personality tests		
	Aptitude tests			Aptitude tests		
	Assessment centre • Tests/mix			Assessment centre • Tests/mix		

* Add rows as necessary

** Delete methods not used in the original or revised plan.

In each case you may have been creative in your thinking and considered several ways of reaching a target audience and some simple, effective selection methods. Of course, you may have realised why the common methods of marketing and selection are so popular: there is good reason for using standard methods of marketing and selection!

Activity 1 Option B outputs

Either

- *A completed version of Table 10.6.*
- *A version of Table 11.2 (the table will be amended in Activity 2).*

Or

- *A version of Table 10.6 with the final column incomplete.*
- *A completed version of Table 11.2 (the table will be amended in Activity 2).*

Reading 5

Reading 5, *Ethics in recruitment and selection*, in Chapter 9 may help you to improve your recruitment and selection plan. It explores in more detail issues of fairness that should be considered when recruiting. When reading this text think about the last time you were recruited to a new role – were these ethical guidelines followed? How would you have felt if they were not? Also consider what you planned in Activity 1: are your choices and methods sufficiently fair?

Activity 2

Allow 1 hour for this activity.

Options A and B

In this activity, you will review the recruitment and selection plan you produced in Activity 1 using the 4Es (including ethics) and make improvements to it. The 4Es were covered in Chapter 4. It is always useful to review and improve your work, and this activity provides such an opportunity. Review in particular the advantages and disadvantages columns in your completed version of Table 11.1 and Table 11.2.

Here are some questions to help you:

- Economy: what are the overall costs of your recruitment process likely to be? Are they proportional to the role you are recruiting for? Are you choosing the cheapest advertising and selection methods? If so, have you considered other approaches that may be more effective in the longer term?
- Efficiency: is the method you have chosen the most efficient, given the role you are trying to fill?
- Effectiveness: are the methods you have chosen likely to be effective or are you using methods you have used before but which may not produce the best result?

- Equity: is the design of your recruitment process likely to be fair to all candidates? When organisations are restructuring it is common for vacancies to be for internal applicants only, or more narrowly, for internal candidates whose present jobs are to be removed. When a vacancy is open to both internal and external candidates, will internal candidates have an advantage? In trying to reach your target group through advertising, are you excluding suitable candidates with the methods you use? For example, very local advertisements will normally be seen only by people who live locally.

When you have completed your review consider whether you would change any aspect of the marketing and selection process as a result. Then amend your recruitment and selection plan as necessary. It should now be effective and sufficiently fair, with costs that are proportional to the job.

Finally, seek feedback from a fellow student on your recruitment and selection plan. First, post a message to the Week 11 activity forum containing:

- Your current version of Table 10.5 or Table 10.6.
- A completed and amended version of Table 11.1 or Table 11.2.

The same student may ask you to review his or her work. In either case, consider and comment on the following areas:

- What are the strengths of the approach being taken?
- Are there any problems with the approach taken?
- How would you imagine candidates would feel if they were recruited and selected in this way?
- Have all the necessary cost implications been taken into account?
- Does the recruitment approach seem reasonable bearing in mind the role being recruited?

When you make comments to another student, make sure that they are constructive. If you see strengths, then it is useful to mention these. If you see gaps or proposals that could be improved, it is important that you explain these clearly but positively.

When you have received comments from your fellow student, you can further review your plan and make any final changes you think are necessary.

Providing feedback to another student may have required some thought. You were probably aware of the time your fellow student had spent in developing the plan. Ideally, this awareness will have persuaded you to be constructive, sensitive and balanced. If so it is likely that your feedback was well-received.

Activity 2 Options A and B outputs

- *An amended version of Table 11.1 or Table 11.2.*
- *A contribution to the Week 11 activity forum containing Table 10.5 or Table 10.6 and Table 11.1 or Table 11.2, amended as necessary. The messages must include a request for feedback from another student.*
- *A contribution to the Week 11 activity forum containing feedback to another student on his or her recruitment and selection plan.*

Activity 3

Allow 30 minutes for this activity.

Option A

This activity asks you to compare your (amended) plan with how you were recruited into your current organisation (or if necessary, a previous one). This will provide an opportunity for you to reflect on your own experience of being recruited (good and bad) and gain insight into why recruitment practice can be a key factor in retention of staff.

To carry out the activity, consider:

- The key differences between your recruitment plan and the way that you were recruited.
- Why you think these differences existed.
- The impact that the way you were recruited had on your feelings about the organisation you work for.
- The employee turnover in your organisation (that is, the percentage of staff who leave the organisation, or the part you are most familiar with, each year). Do you feel the recruitment approach plays a role in this?

There is no template for this activity. Identify three key findings or insights and write them in a Word file of about 200 words. This activity is likely to have *looked* easier to carry out than it actually was. You may have found that your plan, if carefully thought out, is an improvement on your experience of being recruited, unless the practices in your organisation are excellent. If they are, then your work in drawing up the plan will have revealed just why the current practices are excellent!

Activity 3 Option A output

- *Three key findings on the differences between your recruitment and selection plan and your own experience of your recruitment and selection.*

Option B

This activity asks you to draw conclusions from your comparison of your recruitment and selection plan with the original one. This will provide an opportunity for you to gain insight into why recruitment practice can be a key factor in retention of staff regardless of whether the case you worked on in Activity 1 was based on an unsatisfactory recruitment and selection process in your own organisation or another one.

To carry out the activity, consider:

- Any key differences between your recruitment plan and the original one.
- Why you think any differences exist.

- The way the person was recruited affected his or her feelings about the employer. (You can do this only if you based Activity 1 on the experience of a person inside or outside the organisation; it will not be possible if you simply reviewed a person specification and recruitment and selection plan.)
- The employee turnover in the organisation (that is, the percentage of staff who leave the organisation each year). Do you feel the organisation's recruitment approach plays a role in this? If you based this activity on the experience of someone outside your organisation, you will need to ask the person about turnover.

There is no template for this activity. Identify three key findings or insights from your comparison of your plan and the original one, and write them in a Word file of about 200 words.

If the recruitment and selection processes and practices in your organisation are excellent, then your work will have revealed just why the current practices are excellent. If not, you may be in a position to control or influence a current, unsatisfactory, recruitment and selection plan – or future recruitment and selection processes – to ensure that new staff have a satisfactory experience. Alternatively, you may have helped a person in an organisation other than your own gain insight into HR practices.

Activity 3 Option B output

- *Three key findings or insights from your comparison of the unsatisfactory recruitment and selection plan, and the new one you created.*

Reading 6

Recruitment and selection is just part of what is known as 'organisational entry'. While it is important to make sure that suitable people are recruited to the organisation, it is equally important that they are helped to understand what is expected of them and that they are helped to establish themselves in the organisation. Reading 6, *Induction and socialisation*, in Chapter 9 deals with these processes. Note that induction – a person's initial transition into the organisation – is something that can be formally arranged. The manager's role will depend to a great extent on the contribution of others, such as HR personnel, and existing systems. Socialisation is the process by which new recruits adapt to the organisation, learning the often unstated 'rules'. As a manager, your role here will be limited, probably to monitoring and discussion. As you read, consider your own context and what is or might be required of you in the induction and socialisation processes.

This week you have covered all the steps in bringing new people into the organisation. What may have struck you is the variety of tasks that need to be carried out, and how all of them, from job design to socialisation, are designed to recruit – and keep – suitable staff who are effective in their jobs.

Week 11 activity outputs

Option A

1 A completed version of Table 10.5.

2 A completed version of Table 11.1, amended as necessary.

3 A contribution to the Week 11 activity forum containing completed versions of Table 10.5 and of Table 11.1. The message should contain a request for feedback.

4 A contribution to the Week 11 activity forum containing feedback to another student on his or her recruitment and selection plan.

5 Three key findings on the differences between your recruitment and selection plan and your own experience of your recruitment and selection.

Option B

Either

1 A completed version of Table 10.6.

2 A version of Table 11.2 that is complete expect for column 1 of the Selection method section, amended as necessary.

Or

1 A version of Table 10.6 with the final column incomplete.

2 A completed version of Table 11.2, amended as necessary.

And

3 A contribution to the Week 11 activity forum containing appropriately completed versions of Table 10.6 and Table 11.2. The message should contain a request for feedback.

4 A contribution to the Week 11 activity forum containing feedback to another student on his or her recruitment and selection plan.

5 Three key findings or insights from your comparison of your recruitment and selection plan, and the original one.

Learning outcomes

After completing this set of activities and readings you should be able to:

- understand and plan the advertising, shortlisting and selection processes involved in the selection and recruitment of staff
- manage a selection process.

Week 12 Managing performance (1)

Introduction

How can you ensure that the people you manage are working towards organisational goals and that their performance meets your expectations? Managing performance effectively is one of the big challenges in management! This week we explore the processes.

Some people you manage may readily and happily work hard and well, of course – they can be more or less self-managing – while others will need more of your attention. The manager needs to focus both on the tasks being carried out as well as the people who are doing them. Thus, we consider monitoring and supervision. These involve task-oriented activities such as setting realistic goals and people-oriented activities such as supporting individuals and providing feedback successfully.

We then discuss managing poor or declining performance. The readings and activities for this week will prompt you to think about how you manage the performance of those you are responsible for at work and how you might make improvements. The main activity is problem-based and involves investigating and trying to resolve a problem of poor or declining performance.

Week 12 Activities

- Activity 1 Review your own experience of supervising and being supervised. (Allow 30 minutes for this activity.)
- Activity 2 Evaluate your day-to-day performance management of staff you are responsible for. (Allow 90 minutes for this activity.)
- Activity 3 Identify, analyse and work out a solution to a case of poor or declining performance. (Allow 2 to 3 hours for this activity.)

Readings

All readings are in *Managing and managing people*, Chapter 10 'Managing performance'.

- Reading 1 The performance management cycle
- Reading 2 Day-to-day performance management: supervision and monitoring
- Reading 3 Giving feedback on performance
- Reading 4 Managing poor or declining performance

Activity 1

Allow 30 minutes for this activity.

This activity asks you to review a supervisory relationship you have, or have had, with a line manager. This is a relationship with your line manager in which you meet to discuss your progress and review objectives or goals on a regular basis and not just at the yearly appraisal.

You may not have been in a supervisory relationship: for example, because you are self-employed; or you may have infrequent discussions with your line manager about your performance. If this is so, then consider these discussions in terms of the information and support your line manager provided. In either case, focus on what works (or worked) well and what does or did not. Then consider how the way in which the supervision or discussions have shaped your own relationship with those you manage. Be as honest as you can: you may well be basing your behaviour on poor practice as well as good practice! The activity is designed to help you think about the way you manage performance.

Use Table 12.1 to structure your output. You may be fortunate in having a line manager who has very good practices, who has established a good relationship with you and who has adapted their style to your needs. In this case, you will have a good role model on which to base your own practices. However, in some cases, you may have more experience of managing the performance of others than your line manager has, or have better practices, perhaps from working in another organisation or department. In these cases, how your performance was managed may have helped you to avoid managing staff performance in the same way as your own line manager does. Your experiences will necessarily have shaped your behaviour.

Table 12.1 Performance management review

The supervisory relationship (or other relationship)	Describe the frequency and usual content of the meetings/discussions Say whether the meetings/discussions help to establish (and if they help to maintain) a good working relationship
Content of the meetings/discussions that helped my performance	Up to three examples
Content of the meetings/discussions that did not help my performance	Up to three examples
Three important ways in which these meetings/discussions have shaped the way I manage the performance of others	

You were probably already aware of what in your own line manager's approach to performance management is helpful, and what is not helpful. But how easy was it to think about the influence on your own practice as a manager of others? Perhaps you have already begun to think about the ways in which you (and perhaps your line manager!) can improve your management of others. This will be useful for Activity 2.

Activity 1 output

- *A completed version of Table 12.1.*

Readings 1, 2 and 3

Now read *The performance management cycle, Day-to-day performance management: supervision and monitoring* and *Giving feedback on performance*. All these are in Chapter 10.

Reading 1, *The performance management cycle*, introduces the stages in performance management and the different types of tasks that, ideally, a manager needs to carry out. These are: task-centred and people-centred activities. Consider your own context as you read: do you go through all the stages? Do you carry out all the activities?

The second reading, *Day-to-day performance management: supervision and monitoring*, considers supervision and monitoring and outlines common approaches for each. Note the differences between supervision and monitoring. There is more on supervision than on monitoring in this reading because many monitoring processes have already been covered in Week 4. Guidelines are provided for setting up and managing the supervision of those you manage and for monitoring their progress. How would you rate yourself on supervisory and monitoring tasks?

Reading 3, *Giving feedback on performance*, focusses both on giving and receiving feedback. Both are important for improving performance. As a manager you will receive feedback on your own performance from more senior staff and perhaps from members of your team or work group. Learning to receive feedback is as important as learning to give it. Overreacting or being defensive will not encourage people to give you good quality feedback that is helpful to you. Thinking about how it feels to receive feedback often helps people to improve their skill at giving feedback.

Activity 2

Allow 90 minutes for this activity.

For this activity you are asked to evaluate your day-to-day performance management of staff you are responsible for. As the staff you manage are likely to have different needs, base the activity on three people you manage (or all the staff you manage if there are fewer than three). The purpose of this activity is to conduct a self-assessment of how you manage the performance of others, and to indicate what you will change as a result of what you have learned from this week's first three readings.

Use Table 12.2 for your output. It has columns for you to indicate the activities you carry out when discussing or supervising the performance of the staff members you identify, and for assessing whether and how well you carry out each activity listed. Then you are asked to make a general assessment of your performance. To do this, consider the activities you do and do not do, or do best and less well. Is there a pattern? Do you concentrate more on task-focussed activities or more on person-focussed activities? Is this because you are more interested in one type of activity, or because you are responding to the person or context?

Finally, having identified your strengths and weaknesses, and made an overall assessment, identify the activities that you need to do more of, or more often, both in general and with each of the three people you chose. It is useful to specify how and when these activities will be done (unless as part of routine discussion/supervision meetings) and to say why you think the activities you have selected will improve performance in your context.

If you have no current staff management responsibilities, then base the activity on a previous role in which you did have this responsibility. Alternatively, assess your line manager in relation to the management of your own performance and use the results of the activity to discuss your needs with your manager. Describe how you will approach the discussion and provide feedback. Adapt Table 12.2 accordingly and create a new section: 'Approach to discussion and framing of feedback'. Decide whether to have the discussion with your manager. It would be a good opportunity to practisc your feedback techniques.

Table 12.2 Performance management self-assessment

Task-focussed activities	**Person 1**	**Person 2**	**Person 3**	**Whether I carry out this activity and how well I do it**
Shaping – structuring the task				
Target setting				
Explaining				
Delegating				
Guiding				
Limiting				
Negotiating				
Resourcing				
People-focussed activities	**Person 1**	**Person 2**	**Person 1**	**Whether I carry out this activity and how well I do it**
Coaching				
Encouraging				
Facilitating				
Counselling				
Rewarding				
Representing				
Evaluating				

Overall self-assessment

Activities I will do more of (and, if not done in discussions/supervision meetings, how and when) and why I think each will improve/maintain performance:

In general:
Specifically:
Person 1
Person 2
Person 3

The most difficult part of this task was likely to have been assessing your overall performance in managing the performance of others. You may have been surprised to find more strengths than you expected, or disappointed to find weaknesses. It is often useful to discuss a self-assessment with a trusted colleague who knows your work well to see if your view matches theirs. In specifying the activities you need to do more of, or more frequently, it might have been hard in some cases to give context-specific reasons why you think the activities you have selected will improve the performance of others. However, occasional coaching might have a particular benefit in your work context or for a specific member of staff. A logical next step in Activity 2 would be for you to devise a SMART plan to implement the improvements you identified, or to devise and implement a new overall plan for managing the performance of those who report to you. As a manager who is studying in order to be more effective, however, you are likely to do this anyway.

Activity 2 output

- *A completed version of Table 12.2.*

Reading 4

Reading 4, *Managing poor or declining performance*, in Chapter 10 deals with the difficult problem of poor or declining performance in a person who we are responsible for at work. There are various options for addressing this. Each has advantages and disadvantages which must be assessed carefully. Decisions will normally depend on the situation. As you read, try to think of a situation in which a person's performance is poor or has declined. This will help you prepare for Activity 3 which is problem-based.

Activity 3

Allow 2 to 3 hours for this activity.

In this activity you will identify, analyse and plan the solution to a problem of poor or declining performance in a person you manage. It may be a situation that has just started or one you have delayed dealing with. Use Table 12.3 to structure your output. It contains advice and questions to guide you. Note that you may have to gather information about the poor or declining performance in order to decide on a solution. This may involve discussing with the person any particular difficulties they may have been experiencing.

You can base the activity on a previous case of poor or declining performance that you had to manage, but try to plan a solution that might have been more effective than the one you chose then. Alternatively, choose a person who is underperforming and act as if you were the person's line manager. However, you may not have sufficient information unless you know the person well or work closely with them. You could also base the activity on your own experience if, at some time recently, you were underperforming. Then you could base your solution on the action that an informed manager might take. However, additional care is required when analysing the problem and its possible causes: it is very easy to make incorrect assumptions or take a biased view.

Note that the main options for solutions are set out for you in Reading 4 *Managing poor or declining performance.* To decide among options, you will need to draw on the information you gathered during your analysis. The options of moving the employee to another job in the organisation, or ending their work in the organisation are not included and we recommend that you do not use these two options in the main part of your activity. This is because these options would normally be considered only if performance failed to improve as a result of other efforts.

Table 12.3 Resolving the problem of poor or declining performance

Problem identification and description	To identify a problem to resolve, consider: Who is underperforming? What is the person's job and the context? To whom is this a problem and why? Are there any other impacts?
Analysis	Analyse the situation by considering: What are the symptoms of poor or declining performance or how did you recognise it? What might the causes be? Consider all possibilities including performance management, motivation, equipment, resources, and so on. Draw on any part of the module you have studied so far. Talk to the person concerned, if possible, and explore any current difficulties they may be having with their work. You do not have to address the issue of performance directly if it is not convenient or appropriate at this time. What problems arise because of the poor or declining performance? Set out any gaps in your analysis. State any assumptions you have had to make, and draw on relevant module themes.
Conclusions to the analysis	Interpret your findings, referring to any important causes of the problem and significant features of your analysis. Prepared to conclude that the poor or declining performance is caused by technical, motivational, personal, or other problems. Often a problem is due to more than one cause, or there may be a primary cause – for example, lack of training – which then produces a secondary cause, demotivation.

Table 12.3 continued

Recommendations	Set out criteria for a solution, recognising any constraints, which may include organisational ones. Consider the options: take no action; act to correct performance; revise the standards set. If the person who is underperforming is a member of a team, consider the impact of each option on the team. Make a choice, justify it and briefly set out how you will go about the option you have chosen. Write these as SMART recommendations or as an action plan. In the case of Option 1 (take no action), will you set a date or a performance level, after which you will consider taking action? Note that your recommendations or action plan will probably be short and tentative: implementing the plan would create opportunities for gathering more information that might result in amendments to your plan. Thus, treat your first plan as part of the process of solving the underperformance problem. State any assumptions you have had to make. Use module concepts and make sure you address any relevant module themes such as ethics.
Advantages, disadvantages and implications	Set out the advantages and disadvantages of the particular option you have chosen and particular recommendations/plans you have made. Consider the implications of your chosen option and your particular solution or plan. If necessary, suggest plans to overcome or reduced disadvantages and negative implications – or return to an earlier stage in the problem-solving process if a disadvantage or implication is too impactful and cannot easily be overcome.

Confronting poor performance is never easy, unless the cause is straightforward: illness in the family or a police officer's first encounter with a road death. Some cases just resolve themselves as time passes; others require more than personal support to bring about positive outcomes. Even if you decide to do nothing (with good reason), you will have considered the situation carefully and you may have assessed the probability of the person recognising their poor performance and taking corrective action. Alternatively, you may have decided to act, and you will be doing so in a considered and systematic way. This activity may have prompted many thoughts and concerns about how, as a manager, you can deal with some of the most sensitive and difficult areas in managing people. We also hope the activity has shown you that you can deal with these areas of management in a straightforward way.

Activity 3 output

- *A completed version of Table 12.3.*

Week 12 activity outputs

1 A completed version of Table 12.1.

2 A completed version of Table 12.2.

3 A completed version of Table 12.3.

Learning outcomes

After completing this set of activities and readings you should be able to:

- understand how to manage performance and what tasks and skills are required for day-to-day monitoring and supervision
- understand your own performance management practices in managing the performance of others and identify areas for improvement
- know how to give and receive feedback effectively
- recognise and know how to address poor or declining performance.

Week 13 Managing performance (2)

Introduction

When were you last involved in a performance appraisal? It is likely that you had your own performance appraised, or that you appraised the performance of people you manage, during the last year, particularly if you work for a large organisation. If we had asked this question a few years ago your answer might have been different. In some smaller organisations performance appraisals can be infrequent but, in general, they are now a regular event in many organisations. In order for appraisals to be useful and constructive to all those involved, managers need to be knowledgeable about the appraisal process. While we often associate appraisals with the appraisal interview, preparing for the interview or meeting and providing support to staff before and after the formal event are equally important. Managers have to support and appraise staff against objectives, often in the midst of changing organisational targets and circumstances, personal issues in individual's lives, and people leaving and joining teams.

In Week 12 we looked at setting objectives, monitoring progress and supervising employees on a day-to-day basis. This is only one part of managing the performance management cycle, however. This week we look more specifically at the appraisal process. We focus on collecting evidence, preparing, and conducting an appraisal interview or meeting. The main activity is problem-based and focusses on analysing the appraisal system and processes in the organisation you work for (or your part of it) and recommending or planning improvements.

Week 13 Activities

- Activity 1 Reflect on your own experiences of being appraised. (Allow 1 hour for this activity.)
- Activity 2 Investigate appraisal guidelines in your organisation. (Allow 1 to 2 hours for this activity.)
- Activity 3 Prepare a report to the HR director (or equivalent) with SMART recommendations on the improvement of current appraisal systems. (Allow 3 hours for this activity.)

Readings

All readings are in *Managing and managing people*, Chapter 10 'Managing performance'.

- Reading 1 Performance management and the appraisal process
- Reading 2 Preparing for the appraisal process
- Reading 3 Conducting the appraisal meeting

Activity 1

Allow 1 hour for this activity.

There are two options for this activity, depending on whether you have had the experience of having your work performance appraised. Choose Option 1 if you have this experience and Option 2 if you do not.

Option 1 If you have experienced being appraised

Think about your own experiences of being appraised. Being aware of your own appraisal can help you to develop the skills to appraise others effectively. It can also help to identify problems in the appraisal system in the organisation you work for, or in your part of it, or in other organisations where you have worked. The activity provides an opportunity for you to compare your experiences with those of other students. First, consider your experiences of appraisal in your present job or in a previous one. Use Table 13.1 for your output.

Table 13.1 Experience of appraisal

How often is your performance appraised?
Who appraises it?
How do you prepare for the appraisal?
What does being appraised feel like – before, during and afterwards?
What are the benefits of appraisal for yourself (the appraisee), the appraiser (for example, your manager) and the organisation as a whole?
Other thoughts on the process.
Summary (about 200 words).

Now post your summary to this week's activity forum. Read the contributions of other students and compare your summary with those of at least two other students. The contributions may refer to Option 1 or Option 2 (where there is no formal appraisal process). We suggest you look at examples of both, if possible. What similarities and differences do you note? Write the main similarities and differences in three key points in a Word file in about 100 words.

At its best, appraisal can be mutually rewarding for the appraiser and the appraisee and an important developmental event for the person being appraised. At its worst, emotions can run high and a fair and accurate assessment of performance is not made. If your experiences were mostly of the first type, then you will have been able to draw on examples of good practice which you can and may already use. If your experiences were mostly of the second type, then you can put these to good use, if you have not done so already, by making sure your own staff do not experience the same thing!

Activity 1 outputs (Option 1)

- *A completed version of Table 13.1.*
- *A contribution to the Week 13 activity forum containing your summary.*
- *Three key points summarising the main similarities and differences between your own experience and those of at least two other students.*

Option 2 If you have NOT had the experience of being appraised

The purpose of this activity is to identify the ways in which your work performance is currently reviewed and supported so that in a later activity, you can consider whether any benefit could be gained by adding effective formal appraisal to the existing performance management system.

First, consider the ways in which your performance is reviewed in your present job (or in a previous one). Use Table 13.2 for your output.

Table 13.2 Experience of performance review and support

How often is your performance reviewed?
Who reviews it?
How do the reviews work? (What forms do they take and how formal are they?)
How well do these reviews work?
How are your work objectives set?
How do you receive support, if it is ever needed?
What are the benefits of your work being reviewed and supported in this way?
What are the disadvantages of your work being reviewed and supported in this way?
Summary (about 200 words)

Now post your summary to this week's activity forum. Read the contributions of other students and compare your summary with those of at least two other students. The contributions may include Option 1 or Option 2 (where there is no formal appraisal process). We suggest you look at examples of both, if possible. What similarities and differences do you note? Write the main similarities and differences in three key points in a Word file of about 100 words.

Performance review and support can be excellent without the formality of an annual appraisal: much depends on the work context. Sometimes, in a small close-knit team, good day-to-day performance management processes work well. But when you are a manager, often your own line manager does not work as closely with you as you do with members of your team or work group. Thus, you may have identified some disadvantages. These might be that there is no formal opportunity for work objectives to be set, for assessing learning and development needs or for receiving systematic feedback from people other than your line manager.

Activity 1 outputs (Option 2)

- *A completed version of Table 13.2.*
- *A contribution to the Week 13 activity forum containing your summary.*
- *Three key points summarising the main similarities and differences between your own experience and those of at least two other students.*

Reading 1

Now read Reading 1, *Performance management and the appraisal process*, in Chapter 10. This reading explains how appraisal fits into the wider on-going system of performance management. It sets out the advantages of having well-developed and implemented performance management systems in place for both the individual employee and the organisation – and some reasons why appraisals may go wrong.

Activity 2

Allow 1 to 2 hours for this activity.

This activity asks you to investigate and identify the performance management policies and practices in your organisation, or your part of it. They are likely to include systems for day-to-day monitoring and supervision, which you read about last week, and may include an appraisal process. Looking at your organisation's policies will give you an understanding of what the organisation considers ideal. When you identify the practices you will find out what actually happens when people are busy and under pressure.

If you work in a large or medium-sized organisation, you will probably be able to find these guidelines on the intranet or in the HR handbook. If you work in a small organisation, you may need to ask your immediate manager. Whatever size organisation you work in, you will have to ask colleagues about their practices. Allow time for this. Tell them you are seeking information to help you with your management studies and that the information thcy givc you will rcmain confidcntial (only you and your tutor will see it). Avoid being judgemental about any practices, regardless of how you feel about them. Listen actively and ask open questions! (Remind yourself how to do this by quickly re-reading parts of Chapter 2 on communication.) If necessary, you can base the activity on an organisation such as a sports club that you belong to. Such an organisation may have full-time or part-time staff and volunteers, or a mixture of these.

Use Table 13.3 for your output for this activity. Identifying policies and practices, whether or not your organisation has an appraisal process, will help you with Activity 3 when you consider improvements to the performance management system.

Table 13.3 Performance management policies and practices

Policies
Day-to-day performance management such as monitoring and supervision
Appraisal process
Practices
Summary (about 200 words) which draws out differences between policies and practices and explains why these might be

How easy it was to get the policy information you needed probably depended on many factors, such as whether your organisation has an HR department and whether policies are documented – and in ways that all members of staff can access. The effort it took to get the information should be of interest to you. It may tell you much about the organisation you work for: for example, the communication climate and culture (the way things are done in the organisation). Finding out about practices should have been a simple matter of talking to other managers, and of considering your own practices. Your comparison between policy and practice may have been revealing: if there were few differences then perhaps there is good leadership and good systems for turning policy into practice. If there were a number of differences you may have been able to identify some reasons for this. Even where an organisation has an HR department, many in the organisation may not think that HR and its 'soft systems' are of any use. Or, good policies may not be implemented properly because of lack of resources, including time. Whatever you found, it is likely to be interesting!

Activity 2 output

- *A completed version of Table 13.3.*

Readings 2 and 3

Reading 2, *Preparing for the appraisal process*, in Chapter 10 covers preparation for appraisals, in particular the collection of evidence and preparing appraisees – for example, by asking them to reflect on their work since their last appraisal. Reading 3, *Conducting the appraisal meeting*, in Chapter 10 sets out what an appraisal meeting might cover and how it might be run.

Activity 3

Allow 3 hours for this activity.

This problem-solving activity asks you to improve whatever system or systems your organisation, or your part of it, has in place for performance management. Systems and processes may or may not currently include monitoring, supervising and appraisal. First, analyse the systems in place and assess how effective they are. Then assess what systems and processes it may be necessary to introduce (and why) to improve performance management. Consider the costs and benefits of potential changes and make recommendations. Your output from Activity 2 will be useful. It would be wise to focus on policy (where policy exists) or practice (where policies do not exist) and what policy changes or changes to practice are needed to improve performance management. If policies (or practices) are absent, then the focus of your analysis will be whether improvements to performance management are needed and whether the introduction of new policies (or practices) is needed. If you found in Activity 2 that practice is not consistent with policy, you may find that trying to resolve the problem is too complex. You might have to consider multiple factors ranging from the policies being insufficiently practical for the context to the policy–practice gap being the result of the structure and culture of the organisation. Planned organisational change may be required – and we have not covered that in the module yet!

If necessary, you can base the activity on an organisation such as a sports club that you belong to. Such an organisation may have full-time or part-time staff and volunteers, or a mixture of these.

When working on this activity, you may want to refer to Week 12's readings on monitoring and supervision. Even after you have described and analysed performance management in your organisation, or your part of it, you may not be able to 'identify the problem' until you have analysed the current policies or practices and their effectiveness or otherwise. Sometimes policies or practices are not flawed individually but they do not produce the desired result when combined or they may not work well with the organisation's other policies and practices. Draw conclusions; work out what the options for improvement are and how feasible they are in your context. Then select one or more, justifying your choices. Make a set of SMART recommendations. Remember to include the advantages, disadvantages and implications of your recommendations. Make clear any assumptions you have made in your analysis and in your recommendations.

From your notes, write a report which includes recommendations to your HR manager, a senior manager or other appropriate person. The report does not have to be presented but should be written as if it is to be presented. Use Table 13.4 for your report, which should be about 750 words long. If you want to structure your notes before you write your report, use the following headings, which should be familiar to you by now:

- Problem identification and description
- Analysis
- Conclusions to the analysis
- Recommendations
- Advantages, disadvantages and implications.

Table 13.4 Report on performance management systems

Cover page	Decide the best person/people to address the report to. Include the title of the report, the addressee(s), author and date.
Summary	Set out the main points of your report including the nature of the problem, your main findings and key recommendations.
Contents	List titles of sections and subsections of the report including the Introduction; give page numbers if you are using them.
Introduction	Start with a brief description of your part of the organisation and your role. Identify and describe the problem, to whom it is a problem and why, and any other impacts. State the purpose of the report. Set out the main assumptions you have made. Mention any ethical, sustainability or climate change issues in the situation being addressed.

Table 13.4 continued

Analysis	Set out the existing situation in the organisation on: (a) supervising and monitoring performance – description; analysis; assumptions (b) appraisal – description; analysis; assumptions. Show what is problematical, or requires improvement in a way that reveals your analysis. If the problem is a complex one, select one or more of the problematic aspects to analyse. Use relevant module concepts, tools and techniques and customised diagrams. Consider and set out in more details any ethical, sustainability or climate change issues. Identify any gaps in your analysis. Set out any assumptions you have had to make in your analysis.
Conclusions to the analysis	Interpret your findings by drawing together the various elements into an overview. Refer to important causes of the problem and significant features of your analysis.
Recommendations	Provide a set of criteria for a solution, recognising any organisational constraints. Set out your SMART recommendations, using module concepts, tools, techniques and customised diagrams for: (a) supervising and monitoring performance (b) appraisal. Make sure you have addressed any ethical, sustainability or climate change issues. If you have had to make further assumptions in your recommendations, say what they are.
Advantages, disadvantages and implications	Assess the benefits and costs of your solution and set out the advantages and disadvantages. Consider any implications of your solution. If necessary suggest plans to overcome or reduce disadvantages and negative implications.
References	Using the Harvard system, set out the sources of the information you used in your report.

Of all the activities relating to performance management, this one is probably the most difficult yet the most satisfying. When studying management we are often made aware of a number of aspects of the organisation we work for. We thought the organisation was running quite satisfactorily but now we realise that it can be improved. This can change the view we have of our employers. But is it highly satisfying when we can see ways of making improvements – ones we can implement – that help us and the people we manage to do our work better, to be more productive. Of course, you may have found that you really do work for an organisation with excellent systems, so that it is very hard to see ways of improving. However, such organisations will often appreciate managers, and indeed all staff, trying to find ways in which the organisation can work better. This will be the case if your organisation has adopted a 'quality culture' (covered later in the module). The theory is: 'Anything that can be done, can be done better!'

Activity 3 output

- *A completed version of Table 13.4.*

Week 13 activity outputs

1. A completed version of Table 13.1 for Option 1 or a completed version of Table 13.2 for Option 2 of Activity 1.
2. A contribution to the Week 13 activity forum containing your summary.
3. Three key points summarising the main similarities and differences between your own experience and those of at least two other students.
4. A completed version of Table 13.3.
5. A completed version of Table 13.4.

Learning outcomes

After completing this set of activities and readings you should be able to:

- understand the purpose of performance appraisal processes
- demonstrate an understanding of appraisal processes, procedures and issues
- conduct an appraisal
- analyse performance management systems and plan improvements.

Week 14 Learning and development at work

Introduction

Day-to-day performance management and appraisal often lead to the need to consider training and development. It is usually necessary to choose from several good ways (or available ways) in which people can learn new skills and improve existing ones, or develop themselves, in order to enhance their performance. Although, in large organisations, staff training and development is often a function of the HR department, managers have a role to play because of the emphasis on individual needs and individual learning. Managers will be involved in identifying learning and development needs with individual staff members, and in providing support. This may include providing opportunities for a new skill to be applied or meeting learning needs directly if what needs to be learned is best organised 'locally,' for example, by coaching or observation.

This week we consider how you can support the work-based learning and development of those you manage. We consider the nature of work-based knowledge and learning, the relationship between individual learning and the organisation and the importance of organisational attitudes towards work-based learning. Ways of turning everyday experiences into learning opportunities are explored, together with identifying learning needs and ways in which they can be met.

The main activities for this week are to review learning and development opportunities and support in your organisation, or your part of it, or your work group, conduct a learning needs analysis and make recommendations for improvements to learning and development provision and support.

Week 14 Activities

- Activity 1 Identify the learning and development opportunities and support in your organisation and exchange notes on these opportunities with other students. (Allow 1 hour for this activity.)
- Activity 2 Write a report on the training and development needs of your work group, how these needs can or cannot be met and how the provision of training and development can be improved. (Allow 3 to 4 hours for this activity.)

Readings

All readings are in *Managing and managing people*, Chapter 11 'Learning and development at work'.

- Reading 1 The need to learn
- Reading 2 Knowledge and adult learners

- Reading 3 Learning from everyday experiences
- Reading 4 Identifying learning needs
- Reading 5 Learning and development activities
- Reading 6 Evaluating learning (optional)

Readings 1 and 2

The first two readings in Chapter 11 set out the key principles and concepts. Reading 1, *The need to learn*, sets out what drives learning in organisational settings and illustrates some different forms of informal and formal learning. It also considers the way in which some organisations prioritise learning and development (and why) to produce a culture of learning.

Reading 2, *Knowledge and adult learners*, covers the different types of knowledge that may need to be acquired. Learning in adulthood, individual differences and barriers to learning are considered. To help you with the activities that follow, as you read, consider and make notes on three areas in particular. These are the different types of learning that take place in your own organisation (or your part of it, or your work group), the importance the organisation you work for attaches to learning and development at work, and individual attitudes towards learning and development.

Is there a connection between individual attitudes and the way the organisation deals with staff learning and development? Does it 'do what is necessary' or does it positively encourage learning and development? If it encourages learning and development, how does your organisation do this? Why does it do this? How does it benefit? The organisation's attitude to learning and development may be important if you want to improve training and development opportunities for the staff you are responsible for.

Activity 1

Allow 1 hour for this activity.

For this activity you are asked to identify training and development opportunities and learning support in your workplace. The five steps in this activity are set out briefly and then further guidance is given.

1. Identify learning opportunities in the organisation you work for, or your part of it, or your work group (and you), and decide whether these opportunities are formal or informal. We suggest that you consider an area with fewer than 30 employees.
2. Identify the ways in which these learning opportunities are supported by the organisation, by you as a manager and by staff members or members of your work group.
3. Identify any barriers to learning and development. Consider not only time and cost, but the attitudes of the organisation and individuals towards learning and development.

4 Draw a conclusion about the learning and development opportunities.
5 Post your completed activity to this week's activity forum and read the contributions of other students.

This activity will help you with Activity 2 when you address improvements to learning and development in your workplace.

Use Table 14.1 for your output. When completing the table, summarise opportunities and methods of support as categories and provide at least one example for each category. Take care to focus on the opportunities and support relevant to your work group or area of responsibility.

Further guidance

Note that learning and development support by the organisation is not just the provision of training and development. Consider whether the organisation pays for it, allows employees to learn or train in work time, reduces their normal work while they are learning, evaluates the learning and training, follows up progress, and so on. Your support as a manager may include most of these, but it may also include creating opportunities for a person to apply new skills, making allowances while a person is learning a new skill (additional time, lower work standards), and providing encouragement and support. Support by work-group members may simply involve providing encouragement. However, it may extend to helping a person learn and practise a new skill, and being tolerant of mistakes.

You may need to do some research on learning and development opportunities by asking more senior managers or the HR department if your organisation has one. Allow time if you need to do this. If you need to conduct some research, it may also tell you something about potential barriers to learning and development for members of your work group (and for you). Note that informal opportunities for learning and development may be provided in practice (and supported) but not documented or formally recognised (for example, by good practice guidelines). You will know already what informal opportunities you, as a manager, provide for work-group members. If you currently provide none, then you can ask colleagues what kinds of informal opportunities they provide for their staff. If your organisation has an HR department, you can ask what kinds of informal learning and development the organisation supports. You might also ask about barriers to learning and development: try to go beyond time and cost.

Finally draw a conclusion about the learning and development opportunities relevant to your area of responsibility or your work group and you.

The activity will be relevant even if the organisation you work for (or belong to) is a not-for-profit enterprise with very few full-time or part-time staff and many volunteers: voluntary work requires training and support and some volunteers are likely to be volunteering in order to broaden their personal development. In the UK, it is common for voluntary organisations to be offered staff training services by other not-for-profit organisations, so your research may take you outside the organisation. If necessary base the activity on an organisation with which you are very familiar or with which you are associated: for example, a leisure club or a political or religious association which has full-time or part-time staff and volunteers. You will need to base the remaining activities for this week on the organisation you choose at this point, so be sure that you are sufficiently familiar with the organisation and those who work for it, or volunteer for work in it.

When you have completed Table 14.1 post a copy of it to the Week 14 activity forum. In your message, include some details of the organisation to which you are referring. The contributions of other students will help you with the remaining activities this week – and your contribution will help them.

Table 14.1 Learning and development opportunities and support

Sector, purpose, size and types of work that the part you are responsible for does, or that your work group is engaged in:
Learning opportunities available in the organisation you work for, or your part of it, or those opportunities that are available to your work group, whether formal or informal (categories and examples):
The ways in which these are supported:
By you (categories and examples):
By work-group members (categories and examples):
Barriers to learning and development (categories and examples):
Conclusion

You may have been surprised either positively or negatively at the training and development opportunities offered by your organisation. You may also have realised that time and support given by you and your work-group members constitute a great deal of, often informal, training and support provision. However, if you work in a highly regulated sector where the government requires a range of training you may see significant differences between your own and other students' postings. Training and development should not be judged by the number of training courses offered: off-the-job training in the form of short courses, particularly in so-called soft skills, can be ineffective. This is more likely when courses are not provided at the right time and the appropriate support is not given afterwards. Having assessed how much you and your work group can provide, you can probably see what might prevent you from offering more.

Activity 1 outputs

- *A completed version of Table 14.1.*
- *A contribution to the Week 14 activity forum containing a completed version of Table 14.1 and details of the organisation referred to.*

Readings 3, 4 and 5

These readings will help you to build on Activity 1 and to complete Activity 2.

Reading 3, *Learning from everyday experiences*, in Chapter 11 outlines two types of theories of work-based learning: experiential learning and reflective learning. Note that neither type of learning is likely to happen without some effort and discipline, despite some claims that such learning happens naturally in adults. It may do at times, but we can probably all think of instances when learning at work is based on trial and error. Note that asking why something has happened is the key to learning and to reframing our understanding of something. This is probably the most important feature of conscious learning.

Reading 4, *Identifying learning needs*, in Chapter 11 has two tools for conducting a learning needs analysis. The first can be used in any context. The second applies more to people in professional roles and involves individuals in identifying and seeking to meet learning and development needs over a period of time as part of continuing professional development (CPD) and career planning. You may already have a professional development plan, of which this module may be part.

Reading 5, *Learning and development activities*, in Chapter 11 covers some common ways of providing training and development at work, excluding formal, specialist courses. The suitability of each will depend on what is being learned. Note that some require considerable commitment, although these methods tend to be self-directed and used among professionals. Are all the methods familiar to you? Might any be useful, even if they need adaptation? Do not forget that coaching and mentoring – two very popular methods of learning and development – were covered in Week 8 but are relevant here.

Reading 6 (optional)

To decide whether you need to study Reading 6, *Evaluating learning*, in Chapter 11 at this point, look at what is required for Activity 2. If your circumstances fit the first situation listed in Activity 2, you can simply indicate the value of evaluation. If your circumstances fit the second it might be useful to suggest some simple and general ways in which the effectiveness of what you are suggesting can be assessed. If your circumstances fit the third example, then the content of *Evaluating learning* will be particularly useful to you in the activity. Evaluating learning is important because it can help you to improve training and development so that the needs of learners and the organisation are met better. The reading sets out two models of evaluation: decide for yourself which is more useful in different circumstances. Whenever you are involved in training and development, you will be responsible for particular aspects of it. Simple forms of evaluation can usually be done in the course of work and can help you to systematically carry out these responsibilities. Thus, if you do not read *Evaluating learning* at this point, return to it when you have time, or when you are working on your ECA.

Activity 2

Allow 3 to 4 hours for this activity.

This activity is problem-based. Your task is to carry out a training and development needs analysis for your work group, or those staff you are responsible for, and, on the basis of Activity 1, consider whether these needs can be met effectively. Then make recommendations to improve provision of training and development so that these needs can be met. Include your own learning and development needs in your analysis.

Circumstances can vary considerably in different organisations. Some possible ones are set out below with, where necessary, the assumptions you might make so that you can carry out the activity.

1. You do not have an appraisal system in place. The activity should be straightforward for you to carry out in this situation.
2. The training and development needs of your work group were identified and agreed in principle during the appraisal meetings but not in detail. This could be because you have not yet looked at budgets, or at suitable or available methods. The activity will be straightforward for you to carry out but you will need to focus more on how training and development needs can best be met. You may want to read Reading 6, *Evaluating learning*, so that you can outline how you would evaluate the training and development you are setting out in your recommendations.
3. Your organisation considers itself to have a comprehensive training and development plan in place, and/or all the work-group members have professional development plans. Assume here that needs that cannot be met are often not recorded and that some provisions can be improved. Thus, your focus will be to see if needs are being met effectively. You may want to include in your recommendations for improvements some proposals for evaluating effectiveness. The issues raised in Reading 6, *Evaluating learning*, will help you to make an initial assessment of effectiveness.

In each case, use the questionnaire set out in Reading 4, *Identifying learning needs*, as a basis for discussion with members of your work group. If the work group you manage is large, base your analysis on a sample of up to four employees with different needs. Discussion is best, because you will be able to assess individual learning experience and learning skills.

It will be important to explain to those you approach that you are *exploring* how the organisation meets training and development needs. You will need to manage their expectations so that they do not think you are about to meet all their training and development needs or wants. Match the time you have available to the scale of the exploration you are planning. You may be able to carry out the audit as part of your managerial activities.

When you have gathered and considered the training and development needs, and assessed the benefits of these needs being met, consider *how* best they can be met given the type of skills needed and the individuals who require them. Is the usual way to meet a need the most appropriate one? Consider the various training and development methods you have covered (including coaching and mentoring), and informal learning. Which methods fit which needs best? Now consider whether your organisation provides – or supports – any of these. Consider whether you can provide and support one or more appropriate methods. Consider the support the others in the work group can give. Now consider the barriers: the learning culture of the organisation, cost and time, for example. Then consider which barriers can be removed or reduced and how.

You should now be in a position where you have matched some learning needs to existing provision. Where you have needs that you cannot match to existing provision, recommend the kinds of provision and support that you think your organisation should offer (or allow managers and staff to offer). Alternatively, recommend changes to existing provision so that needs can be better met. Recommend what you would like to (and could) offer and what you want formal support for; for example, introducing personal development plans, or coaching. Recommend what you want the organisation to support in terms of mutual help colleagues might give one another. Here, it would be a good idea to look at the activity forum and see what provisions and support other organisations offer. Note that even in an organisation with a culture of learning, some forms of help may not exist, or may not be used for various reasons but might be if they were adapted or better rewarded or regarded. Further, there may be room for the improvement of training and development activities and some learning practices so that they are more effective. If you work for an organisation with such a culture, consider all the elements that can reduce the effectiveness of learning using the material in Reading 6, *Evaluating learning*.

In all cases, be clear about how any existing barriers might be removed or reduced (or recommend evaluation to more fully identify them). Some barriers and possible solutions may be quite obvious. For example, if staff are unwilling to help one another because their performance is assessed against targets, can the targets be adjusted when one person is helping to train another? Could an appraisal criterion be 'citizenship' – being a good citizen in the organisation by helping others to become more skilled? Rewarding desirable behaviour is usually the best way of ensuring that it happens, but the overall benefits need to outweigh the costs for the organisation. Some reasons will be less clear and will require further investigation, which you should include in your recommendations.

We are not asking you to consider how your plans can be resourced, because in most cases you are limiting your activity to a sample from the work group. We suggest you assume that the plans would be cost-effective in improving your work group's performance and would be resourced.

Finally, write a report of about 750 words, addressed to your HR director or a senior manager setting out your case for improving training and development provision in the organisation and your recommendations. You do not have to send the report, of course. Table 14.2 is provided to help you structure your report.

Table 14.2 Report on training and development provision and support

Cover page	Include the title of the report, addressee(s), author, date.
Summary	Set out the main points of your report including the nature of the problem, your main findings and key recommendations.
Contents	List titles of sections and subsections of the report including the Introduction; give page numbers if you are using them.
Introduction	Start with a brief description of your part of the organisation and your role. Identify and describe the problem, to whom it is a problem and why, and any other impacts. State the purpose of the report. Set out the main assumptions you have made. Mention any ethical, sustainability or climate change issues in the situation being addressed.
Analysis	You might begin by considering the existing provision and support in the organisation (formal, informal, etc.) Show what is problematical, or requires improvement in a way that reveals your analysis. In your analysis you are likely to be attempting to identify gaps in existing provision and support needs of the work group, and the types of learning and development required. Consider why these gaps might exist, such as barriers to learning and development in the organisation If the problem is a complex one, select one or more of the problematic aspects to analyse. Use relevant module concepts, tools and techniques and customised diagrams. Consider and set out in more details any ethical, sustainability or climate change issues. Identify any gaps in your analysis. Set out any assumptions you have had to make in your analysis.
Conclusions to the analysis	Interpret your findings by drawing together the various elements into an overview. Refer to important causes of the problem and significant features of your analysis.

Table 14.2 continued

Recommendations	Provide a set of criteria for a solution, recognising any organisational constraints. Set out your SMART recommendations, using module concepts, tools, techniques and customised diagrams for: (a) new or improved types of training and development provision and support (formal/informal). (b) how barriers to learning and development might be removed or reduced. Make sure you have addressed any ethical, sustainability or climate change issues. If you have had to make further assumptions in your recommendations, say what they are.
Advantages, disadvantages and implications	Weigh the benefits and costs of your solution and set out the advantages and disadvantages. Consider and address any implications of your solution. If necessary suggest plans to overcome or reduce disadvantages and negative implications.
References	Using the Harvard system, set out the sources of the information you used in your report.

This activity will have helped you to focus on the learning and development needs of the people you are responsible for, and on your own needs. Unless you lead a professional team of similarly qualified people, you are likely to have identified different training and development needs, different attitudes towards learning, different learning preferences and different learning skills. You will also have established to what extent the organisation can satisfy these needs. Perhaps you realised the value of learning while doing the job and the importance of timeliness. Perhaps you realised that, actually, everyone in the organisation has some responsibility for their own learning, and for supporting the learning of others. Most of all, you may have realised that, provided you have the support of senior managers, there is much you can do to ensure that there is the widest possible range of learning and development opportunities on offer to your staff and that people are well-supported when learning.

Activity 2 output

- *A completed version of Table 14.2.*

Week 14 activity outputs

1 A completed version of Table 14.1.

2 A contribution to the Week 14 activity forum containing a completed version of Table 14.1 and details of the organisation referred to.

3 A completed version of Table 14.2.

Learning outcomes

After completing this set of activities and readings you should be able to:

- understand the need for both formal and informal learning and development at work
- understand what is meant by a culture of learning in organisations
- understand different types of knowledge and how they relate to different aspects of tasks
- understand individual differences in learning skills and preferences
- identify barriers to learning and development at work
- understand the nature of experiential and reflective learning and how these concepts can be applied at work
- identify informal and formal sources of training and development, and support, available in an organisation
- analyse training and development needs and plan improvements in provision and support.

Week 15 TMA 02 preparation

In this week you will prepare your TMA 02.

Week 16 Organisational culture

Introduction

Organisational culture is a term you will see and hear everywhere. Organisations are urged by management consultants to 'create a high-performance culture'. But what is meant by organisational culture? How does it operate? Is it the same throughout the organisation? Can it be changed? As you will see, the concept of organisational culture is an interesting one.

The idea of organisational (or psychological) *climate* is probably more useful for supervisors, team leaders and managers. 'Climate' is about employees' perceptions which a manager can seek to influence in various ways to bring about the benefits associated with a 'good' climate: happier, more-satisfied and more-productive employees.

Week 16 Activities

- Activity 1 Identify the 'culture' of your organisation. (Allow 30 minutes for this activity.)
- Activity 2 Assess the climate within your team. (Allow up to 4 hours for this activity.)
- Activity 3 Plan how to improve the climate to increase performance and employee satisfaction. (Allow 2 to 3 hours for this activity.)

Readings

All readings are in *Managing and managing people*, Chapter 12 'Organisational culture'.

- Reading 1 What is organisational culture?
- Reading 2 Dimensions and types of organisational culture
- Reading 3 Ideal or above-the-norm cultures
- Reading 4 Psychological climate
- Reading 5 Improving the psychological climate: what a manager can do
- Reading 6 What a manager can do to reduce pressure

Readings 1, 2 and 3

How would you describe the way things are done in your organisation? Is everyone expected to follow the rules, do what they are told and check all decisions with their line manager? Or are they expected to set and plan their own goals and pursue them with enthusiasm?

Reading 1, *What is organisational culture?*, in Chapter 12 is a very short reading that sets out what organisational culture is. Reading 2, *Dimensions and types of organisational culture*, in Chapter 12 covers several different ways in which organisational culture has been described and how it might be assessed. As you read, consider your own organisation (and your own part of it) to see if you are able to identify the kind of culture that exists in your organisation (the subject of Activity 1).

Reading 3, *Ideal or above-the-norm cultures*, also in Chapter 12 covers the 'engineering' of organisational cultures – sometimes for continuous quality or performance improvements and sometimes to comply with stringent safety or security needs which may be legal requirements. If you work in a particular sector such as the armed forces, the prison service, nuclear power generation or animal research, then you will be aware that an organisation-wide, systemic approach to safety and security needs to be taken. However, in many other organisations a similar organisation-wide, systemic approach has been taken towards quality, on which the reading focusses. Such a *systemic* approach to operations will affect an organisation's culture. If your organisation does not have such an approach to quality and improvement, you might consider how much the culture of your organisation would have to change, and whether such changes might be beneficial.

Activity 1

Allow 30 minutes for this activity.

In this activity you will try to identify your organisation's culture. If you work for a very large organisation, then choose the parts of it that you know best. Try to consider more than one department, branch or work unit because you may find cultural differences between them. It is not essential that you are accurate: it is more important that you consider the culture and why the organisation might possess this culture. Use Deal and Kennedy's taxonomy based on two dimensions – speed of feedback and uncertainty – and the Handy/Harrison taxonomy based largely on who has power in the organisation. Take into account the culture 'imposed' by your organisation if it has a *systemic* approach to quality, performance, safety or security – that is, if concern for these is fully embedded in systems and practices. Remember, however, that these few dimensions of culture are unlikely to capture fully the culture of your organisation.

First, using Deal and Kennedy's dimensions assess the speed of feedback in your organisation or selected parts of the organisation. Rate speed from 1 (low) to 5 (high). Then assess risk – the uncertainty over outcomes in your organisation or selected parts of the organisation. Rate risk from 1 (low) to 5 (high). Using these ratings, work out where your organisation or your selected parts of the organisation fits on the Deal and Kennedy diagram in Reading 2. If the organisation or any part of it fits right in the middle, it will have elements of all four cultures. Record your assessment in Table 16.1; is your organisation's culture process work hard/play hard, bet your company or tough-guy macho? If you found that selected parts of the organisation had different ratings, and thus different cultures, list each.

When you have done this, assess your organisation or selected parts of the organisation in terms of the Handy/Harrison culture types and list these in Table 16.1. Your assessment here will be less precise and more impressionistic. Finally, make your own brief summary of your organisational culture in about 50 words. Try to cover the following:

1. The extent to which you think the culture is shaped by what the organisation does or different parts of it do, and any 'above-the-norm' factors, such as a systemic focus on quality, performance, safety, security (or any other operational characteristic).
2. Whether power might be distributed differently. This may already have happened as a result of the introduction of total quality management where decisions about improvements often take place at team level.
3. Whether your values are similar to (a) the stated values of the organisation (or selected parts of it) or to (b) those that seem most dominant in the organisational culture(s).
4. One or two advantages and disadvantages of the culture(s) in terms of your everyday managerial work.

Table 16.1 Organisational culture

In terms of Deal and Kennedy's taxonomy of organisational cultures, my organisation/selected parts of the organisation best fit the following culture type(s):
In terms of Handy/Harrison culture types, my organisation/selected parts of the organisation best fit the following culture type(s):
Summary:

If you wish to, you can share the results of Activity 1 with other students in the Week 16 activity forum to see whether particular types of organisation have similar cultures. Be sure to include in your message some details about the organisation you work for.

Thinking about the culture or your organisation or selected parts of it was probably quite difficult. First, we are often too close to be objective. Second, none of the cultures described was likely to be an exact fit. Third, you may have realised that your personal values are not, or not wholly, consistent with those of the organisational culture or different parts of the organisation you may have chosen to look at. This may be the case even if you chose to work for a non-profit organisation because you believe in its mission or purpose. This brief look at the way things are done in your organisation is likely to have raised some issues about what is 'wrong' or frustrating about the culture or cultures – and why change might be difficult.

Activity 1 output

- *A completed version of Table 16.1.*

Reading 4

Reading 4, *Psychological climate*, in Chapter 12 is a very short one that introduces the concept of psychological or organisational climate – the perceptions of employees about what goes on in the organisation, primarily about how they are treated. The important feature to note is that psychological climate can be changed at the level of the work group, although how much will depend at times on the organisational culture. As you read, it would be useful to makes notes on your own perceptions, and whether these are shared by others, in preparation for Activity 2. It is always helpful to try to think of examples that support a perception. Perceptions differ among individuals because our experiences are not identical – and neither are our personalities or the way we view the world.

Activity 2

Allow up to 4 hours for this activity.

In this activity you will assess your perceptions of your organisation, or your part of it, using an inventory devised by Malcolm Patterson and colleagues (2005). You will find the Organizational Climate Measure (OCM) in Module Resources on the module website. Download it now. Also download the document *Scoring and interpreting the Organizational Climate Measure* which you will need in order to complete Activity 2.

Step 1 Completing the questionnaire

You will see that OCM asks for individual perceptions of the organisation. When you complete it, the score will reflect your own views. Thus, if possible, ask at least one or two members of your work group to complete it as well. You will also see that the dimensions covered are not quite the same as those covered in the reading. This is because, over time, researchers have identified many 'climate dimensions', although some are considered to be more important than others. Patterson et al. have adopted a comprehensive, multi-dimensional approach, covering 17 factors – more than in Reading 4. Do not be concerned about this.

If you arrange for members of your work group to complete the questionnaire, please note the particular advice given in Box 16.1.

An alternative to asking work-group members to complete the questionnaire is to use the questionnaire as a framework for discussion. For example, you can ask them how involved they feel when you make decisions that affect them. The point of the activity is not the completion of a questionnaire, but to try to assess the psychological climate. The questionnaire provides a framework for exploration and suggest some questions you might ask. It can help you to identify areas of the psychological climate that might be improved. Make notes for use later in this activity. If you choose this alternative you may wish to read the scoring and interpretation instructions for the questionnaire now, so that you understand what kind of picture of organisational climate it seeks to provide. This may help you to structure your discussion.

Box 16.1 Using the questionnaire

If members of your work group are to complete the questionnaire, make sure that conditions are appropriate for gaining honest and constructive input. Make sure the setting feels relaxed and fairly informal. Explain:

- what you want to do and why
- that you will not be able to address all the issues raised
- that you intend the results to be beneficial to them and to you
- that they do not have to complete the questionnaire if they do not want to.

Ask them to answer the questions in relation to the immediate work group as far as possible – that is, the 'local' psychological climate. It is important that when they respond to questions referring to a supervisor or manager, they are referring to your practices. It is usual to ask individuals to complete the questionnaire without discussion of the questions. After calculating the scores, discuss the results with work-group members and gather their views and suggestions. As there are 17 potential factors to discuss, focus on those that had low scores and over which you have control or influence. Ask, too, what the impact would be if particular climate areas were improved. Remember to treat the views of work-group members and their specific suggestions for improvement not as criticisms of your own practices, but as potential ways of making improvements. Later, discuss your proposals with the work-group members. You will need their support and cooperation if you are to make changes.

Step 2 Scoring and interpreting the questionnaire

Follow the instructions in the document *Scoring and interpreting the Organizational Climate Measure*. Your tutor will provide additional guidance if you need it. When you have calculated the scores and averages for the completed OCM, record them in Table 16.2. If you alone completed the questionnaire, write your score average for each of the 17 scales under 'Score 1'. If you asked one or more other people to complete the questionnaire, write the score average for each scale under 'Score 2'. If you gathered perceptions from work-group members without use of the questionnaire, give each scale you discussed a score that reflects those perceptions and write this under 'Score 3'. Then, whichever method of questionnaire completion you used, provide an average score for each quadrant under 'Overall average score'.

The first part of Table 16.2 is a matrix representing competing values. It allows you to look at the balance between the four competing 'values' discussed in the scoring and interpretation instructions and to assess where the climate lacks balance. Very high scores in one or more quadrants and lower scores in one or more of the others (or vice versa) do not represent balance.

Identify where the lack of balance exists, for example, where the scores in one or more quadrants are low. Alternatively, if there is overall balance, identify scores within a quadrant that are low.

Then consider the individual questionnaire items that make up the scales in the quadrants that lack balance, or the individual scales within quadrants that you found were lower than the others. As a manager, do you have control or influence over any of these? You will address improvement of climate in Activity 16.3. For now, list the most negative and most positive scales in Table 16.2 in the rows indicated. The most positive area may not be the highest scoring quadrant or scale. For example, very high scores for formalisation and tradition (the internal process model) and lower scores in the other three quadrants may reflect perceptions that the organisation is highly controlling with an established bureaucracy in which staff find it difficult to be innovative. However, you might regard high scores for autonomy and staff morale (the HR model) as positive. You will need to use your judgement when identifying positive aspects of the organisational climate. Identifying negative aspects may be more straightforward. Consider why scores on some scales may be low or high. For example, lack of staff training or a high level of reflexivity may be due to pressure from the environment outside the organisation, such as competitive pressure to drive down costs or economic factors that are driving organisational change.

When you have listed what you think are the positive aspects of the climate and what you think are the negative aspects, record briefly in the final row of Table 16.2 any thoughts you may have. For example, do the scores (and balance) reflect your initial perceptions about your organisation or your part of it? Is the climate better or worse than you expected the scores to show? Why might this be? Perhaps, before you completed the questionnaire, one very negative feeling or one very positive feeling about the organisation influenced you before you considered specific factors. Looking at specific and multiple aspects of something usually produces a more balanced and 'rounded' view. If members of your work group completed the questionnaire, differences between their perceptions and your own may be to do with the particular jobs they do, differences in status and so on.

Table 16.2 Organisational climate profile

Flexibility

The Human Relations Model					The Open Systems model				
Scale	**Score**	**1**	**2**	**3**	**Scale**	**Score**	**1**	**2**	**3**
1. Autonomy					1. Innovation and flexibility				
2. Integration					2. Outward focus				
3. Involvement					3. Reflexivity				
4. Supervisory support									
5. Training									
6. Welfare									
	Overall average score:					***Overall average score:***			
The Internal Process Model					**The Rational Goal model**				
Scale	**Score**	**1**	**2**	**3**	**Scale**	**Score**	**1**	**2**	**3**
1. Formalization					1. Clarity of organisational goals:				
2. Tradition					2. Efficiency				
					3. Effort				
					4. Performance feedback				
					5. Pressure to produce				
					6. Quality				
	Overall average Scale:					***Overall average score:***			

Control

Internal focus | External focus

The main negative aspects of the climate	List:
The main positive aspects of the climate	List:
My thoughts in 50 words	

(Source: based on Patterson et al., 2005; Quinn, 1988; Quinn et al., 2007)

While completing the questionnaire you and your work-group members are likely to have had views on how the climate could be improved. In Activity 3 you will consider the negative aspects of the climate over which you have control or influence and what you might do to improve the climate in your work group.

Activity 2 output

- *A completed version of Table 16.2.*

Readings 5 and 6

Reading 3 introduced you to the idea that organisational climate is less difficult to change than organisational culture at the local level. These next two readings will be directly relevant to your managerial work. Reading 5, *Improving the psychological climate: what a manager can do*, and Reading 6, *What a manager can do to reduce pressure*, both in Chapter 12, cover the practical ways in which a manager can improve the psychological climate at a local level. How much of a difference you can make will depend on how supportive the organisation is of the types of behaviours and actions that you want to encourage. However, most organisations are unlikely to object to managers building cohesive work groups in which there is trust and support or to managers dealing with excessive pressure on employees, for example. Happy groups and teams that are satisfying to work in usually mean productive employees. Readings 5 and 6 are designed to help you with Activity 3 – how you might improve the psychological climate in your work group. As you read, keep in mind the results of the organisational climate measure. Make notes on how you might improve the psychological climate in your own work group.

Activity 3

Allow 2 to 3 hours for this activity.

This activity is problem-based, building on the problem-identification and analysis you carried out in Activity 2. The main focus of this activity is to identify and propose what can be done to improve the psychological climate in your work group. If you are responsible for this work group, then develop a set of proposals that you can carry out. If you are not responsible for the work group, develop proposals to present to your line manager. Alternatively, base the activity on how you could contribute to a more positive climate with your colleagues in the work group.

Step 1. First, consider the scores you collected for the Organizational Climate Measure. Consider the balance of values, each scale (and the individual factors that make up each scale if necessary). Identify where improvements can be made in areas over which you or your line manager have influence. While you might not be able to change the traditional ways of senior management, you may control the supervisory support you give, for example. Equally, your line manager may have limited influence in the organisation, but may have control or influence over the degree of autonomy staff have. Among colleagues, open discussion and changes in your behaviour or practices may make a difference.

Step 2. Identify specific problems associated with the scores on these scales or factors, or the ways in which performance, productivity and job satisfaction could be improved. If you have more items on your list than you can deal with, then prioritise by selecting the most important ones. In your choice, take note of what work-group members said about the effects of improving particular areas of the climate. Choose areas that are likely to bring most benefit. Make sure you have control or influence over the 'problem' area even if, in the case of colleagues, your influence is informal. Also check that solving the problem will not create unacceptable conflicts or difficulties, or have effects outside your sphere of influence or control. Look at ways of reducing or removing such difficulties.

Step 3. Using the information provided in Reading 5, *Improving the psychological climate: what a manager can do*, work out what you might do to improve the climate or resolve the problem you identified in Step 2. You can also use the information provided in *Scoring and interpreting the Organizational Climate Questionnaire* on the management roles that may require more emphasis in order to resolve a particular climate problem or make an improvement.

Step 4. Consider the advantages and disadvantages – and implications – of your proposed solution. If your proposal, or aspects of it, require changes to organisational policies or the general culture of the organisation, then they are unlikely to work. You will need to amend your proposal so that the climate factors over which you hope to have an influence are either consistent with organisational policy and culture or have little immediate effect on them. Being supportive, for example, will be noticed by those people who experience an improvement in support but probably not by anyone else.

Step 5. Complete Table 16.3; additional advice is given. Note that it will often be productive to discuss issues or possible remedies with work-group members, particularly if you did not do this during Activity 2. If you line manage members of the work group, getting their input on your own behaviours and actions can be uncomfortable. You may want to read again the short section on receiving feedback in *Giving feedback on performance* in Chapter 10 *Managing performance.*

Table 16.3 Improving the psychological climate

Problem identification and description	Steps 1 and 2 can be used to identify and describe the problem. State to whom it is a problem and why. Mention any other impacts.
Analysis	Step 3 can be used for the problem analysis. Consider: • the questions to which work-group members gave low scores in the area identified • the typical or stated behaviours and actions: for example, supervision is rushed; no time for discussion; manager micro-manages – does not show trust and confidence. Show what is problematical, or requires improvement in a way that reveals your analysis. If the problem is a complex one, select one or more of the problematic aspects to analyse. Use relevant module concepts, tools and techniques and customised diagrams. Consider and set out in more details any ethical, sustainability or climate change issues. Identify any gaps in your analysis. Set out any assumptions you have had to make in your analysis.

Table 16.3 continued

Conclusions to the analysis	Interpret your findings by drawing together the various elements into an overview. Refer to important causes of the problem and significant features of your analysis.
Recommendations	Provide a set of criteria for a solution, recognising any organisational constraints. Set out your SMART recommendations, being sure to include how you will assess whether your aim has been achieved. Use module concepts, tools and techniques. Make sure you have addressed any ethical, sustainability or climate change issues. If you have had to make further assumptions in your recommendations, say what they are.
Advantages, disadvantages and implications	Set out the advantages, disadvantages and implications. Consider: • costs as well as benefits • whether your recommendations are consistent with organisational policy and culture or, at least, have little immediate effect on them • any implications of your solution; if necessary suggest plans to overcome or reduce disadvantages and negative implications.

If you sought the views of others on your own behaviours and actions and on your proposals you probably found that, even while trying to be open to feedback, at times you needed to justify your actions or intentions. Direct reports are sometimes not fully aware of the limits of a manager's influence and control, or time, or pressures from higher in the organisation. (If you developed your proposals for your own line manager, you may have discovered that he or she is subject to demands and constraints that you were not fully aware of.) Thus, you may have to explain why some of the suggestions are not feasible, or why your proposed remedy or remedies are relatively simple. However, small changes have the potential to make a big difference: the size and number of changes is not a good measure of effectiveness.

Understanding organisational culture and climate – and making changes at the work-group level – will prepare you for the last topic of the module, Managing change.

Activity 3 output

- *A completed version of Table 16.3.*

Week 16 activity outputs

1 A completed version of Table 16.1.
2 A completed version of Table 16.2.
3 A completed version of Table 16.3.

Learning outcomes

After completing this set of activities and readings you should be able to:

- understand what organisational culture is
- understand different types of organisational culture and how they might shape the behaviour and processes within organisations and groups
- understand what organisational climate is and how it has an impact on various aspects of work life/performance
- identify organisational climate at a local level, for example, in a team or work group
- identify and plan improvements to the organisational climate.

Week 17 The organisation and the external environment

Introduction

How is the external environment affecting the organisation you work for just now? What will affect it next year? How will your organisation respond? How will this affect what you do as a manager? Environmental scanning – looking outside the organisation at what external factors will have an impact next year or in five years' time – and then looking inside the organisation to see what the impact is likely to be – is one of the main ways in which managers anticipate events and plan for them. It allows managers to be proactive, preparing for action before an event, rather than reactive, that is, taking action after the event.

This week's readings and activities are designed to help you better understand the external environment of your organisation. The main activity asks you to identify different factors in the external environment in which your organisation operates, what opportunities and threats are presented by these factors, and the strengths and weaknesses of your organisation in relation to them. If necessary, you can look at your own part of the organisation, but it will be useful to consider as large a part of the organisation as you can. It can be easy for a manager to say: 'Oh, *that* won't affect us in training and development.' But factors that affect your organisation as a whole will have a direct or indirect affect on every part of it.

Week 17 Activities

- Activity 1 Identify key stakeholders in your organisation. (Allow 90 minutes for this activity.)
- Activity 2 Scan the external environment in which your organisation operates and conduct a SWOT analysis. (Allow up to 5 hours for this activity.)
- Activity 3 Post a contribution on sustainability and climate change to the activity forum and comment on the contribution of others. (Allow 30 minutes for this activity.)

Readings

All readings are in *Managing and managing people*, Chapter 13 'The organisation and the external environment'.

- Reading 1 The external environment
- Reading 2 Stakeholders and their interests
- Reading 3 Understanding the external environment
- Reading 4 Assessing the impact of STEEP factors

Readings 1 and 2

Reading 1, *The external environment*, in Chapter 13 introduces three environments that an organisation operates in: the environment internal to the organisation, the near external environment (suppliers, customers or clients, the local neighbourhood, and so on) and the far external environment full of political, economic and other factors over which we have little or no influence. But can we draw the boundaries between the internal and near external environment in a precise way? Why are they not fixed? As you read, consider the boundaries of the organisation you work for and whether boundary changes are likely.

Reading 2, *Stakeholders and their interests*, in Chapter 13 covers who stakeholders are, their interest in the organisation you work for and how some of the interests of different stakeholders can conflict with one another. As a manager, how do you know who are the important stakeholders? The priority that organisations and managers decide to give particular stakeholders depends on a number of factors. What managers actually do and what it may be *right* to do may be different, however!

Both readings will help you carry out Activity 1. It would also be useful to look again at the section on ethics in the Module Guide.

Activity 1

Allow 90 minutes for this activity.

This activity asks you to identify the key stakeholders of the organisation you work for, to identify their interests and expectations and to conclude which of them should be given priority based first on the descriptive approach that Mitchell et al. (1997) adopt, and then using a normative or ethical approach.

You could consider the whole of the organisation you work for or just the part with which you are familiar, a department, division or group. If necessary, you can base the activity on an organisation you belong to such as a sports club or the parents' association of a school.

The activity is designed to help you think through the concept of stakeholders and their importance for your organisation and for your work. We lead you step-by-step through the activity.

Step 1. Try to identify as many stakeholders of your organisation as you can. You can do this in the form of a list, or if you prefer you could draw a stakeholder map similar to the stakeholder map in Reading 2 (Figure 13.2). When you have identified them, list them in Table 17.1.

Step 2. For each of these stakeholders make an estimate of their power and legitimacy, and the urgency of their claims on your organisation. This is, of course, a somewhat subjective assessment but objective accuracy is not the point here. The important point is how you assess the power, legitimacy and urgency of stakeholders, because it is this assessment that will influence how you deal with them. In column 2 of Table 17.1, indicate their power, legitimacy and/or urgency (low, medium or high).

Step 3. Based on your assessment of power, legitimacy and urgency, decide where the stakeholders you identified are located in the seven categories of stakeholders shown in Figure 13.2 in Reading 2. In column 3, record which category each stakeholder group belongs to (1–7).

Step 4. For the stakeholders you have identified, try to identify their interests in and expectations of your organisation. Note these in column 4 of Table 17.1.

Step 5. From the analysis in Step 3, you will be able to identify the stakeholders who are the highest priority and those who are your lowest priority. Record these in the appropriate row in Table 17.1.

Step 6. Now think again about the priority that each stakeholder group should have for you and your organisation. Instead of using the estimate of power, legitimacy and urgency, think about what normative (ethical) stakeholder theory would have to say about how stakeholder groups should be treated. When you look at their interests and expectations, which ones do you think deserve greatest priority and why? Identify the groups and give your reasons in the appropriate row in Table 17.1.

Step 7. Finally, think about which stakeholder interests you or your organisation could satisfy at the same time. Are they all compatible or are the interests of some stakeholders in conflict with one other? Are there other conflicts between what stakeholders expect – and might be justified to expect from an ethical perspective – and what your organisation needs and is able to do? How would you try to resolve such conflicts?

Here, you need to make a judgement based both on what you know about the capabilities and needs of your own organisation and on what you consider to be an ethically appropriate stance. Record your responses in the last row of Table 17.1.

Table 17.1 Stakeholders' analysis

1 Key stakeholders	**2 Their power, legitimacy and urgency (high, medium, low)**	**3 Stakeholder category**	**4 Stakeholder interests**
1	Power: Legitimacy: Urgency:		
2	Power: Legitimacy: Urgency:		
3	Power: Legitimacy: Urgency:		
4	Power: Legitimacy: Urgency:		

Table 17.1 continued

5	Power: Legitimacy: Urgency:		
6	Power: Legitimacy: Urgency:		
7	Power: Legitimacy: Urgency:		
8	Power: Legitimacy: Urgency:		
9	Power: Legitimacy: Urgency:		

The highest and lowest priority stakeholders, based on Mitchell et al. (1997) are:

The following stakeholders should be given priority on ethical grounds (identify stakeholders and justify why they should be given priority):

Conflict and convergence of interests between different stakeholders and between stakeholders and organisation are:

The stakeholders' interests that can be satisfied at the same time are:

(Source: based on Mitchell et al., 1997)

Parts of this activity may have been difficult if you found that the stakeholders you give, or would give, priority to if you considered their power, legitimacy and urgency are quite different from those you would give priority to on the basis of ethics. It can be uncomfortable to think that the decisions we would make on a hard, business basis are not necessarily the same as those we would make from a moral perspective, or that the organisation we work for is not as ethical as we might like. Equally, if you found conflicting interests and expectations among different stakeholders, it was probably very hard to work out if any of them might be satisfied at the same time. One thing is certain, however, you will be aware of those people and groups who have an interest in the organisation you work for, how difficult it can be to decide who to listen to and to deal with conflicts of interest. Life in organisations is not easy!

Activity 1 output

- *A completed version of Table 17.1.*

Readings 3 and 4

Reading 3, *Understanding the external environment*, in Chapter 13 takes you through the main external factors that influence organisations – the sociological, technological, economic, environmental and political factors, known as the STEEP factors. The reading is longer than the others but you will need the detail on the STEEP factors to help you with Activity 2 in which you will do some 'environmental scanning', that is, attempt to identify factors that will affect your organisation in the near future.

Reading 4, *Assessing the impact of STEEP factors*, also in Chapter 13 sets out how to use two tools to assess the strengths and weaknesses of the organisation you work for in relation to STEEP factors and to identify opportunities and threats that STEEP factors will bring. You will use one of the two tools in Activity 2, and you may want to use the second, too.

Activity 2

Allow up to 5 hours for this activity.

This activity requires you to 'scan' the external environment in which your organisation operates. Again, you can base the activity on the whole organisation or a part of it. It is a substantial activity that will help you consider how the external environment might affect the organisation – what opportunities and threats it might face in the external environment – and what the organisation might do given its strengths and weaknesses. Part of the activity involves identifying these, together with opportunities and threats. Being able to assess external environmental forces is a key aspect of management at every level.

You will need to do some research for this activity. You will need to find out about the impact that factors in the external environment have on your organisation at the moment and what impact they can be expected to have over the next *two years*. Use Table 17.2 for this activity. Step-by-step guidance is given. Each step is labelled in Table 17.2 so you can see where to put your responses.

Step 1. Consider the organisation you work for, the sector in which it operates, its market(s), the raw materials and other resources it needs, and so forth. You can use Figure 13.6 in Reading 4 to help you think about the organisation's primary activities. Now consider those activities on which the external environment has, or is likely to have, an impact. Write these activities in row 1 of Table 17.2 in the columns labelled 1–5. (You can add more columns if needed.) Spend about 30 minutes on this part of the activity. The writable version of this table is in landscape format so that there is more room for your responses.

Step 2. Now consider more carefully the external environmental factors that are having, or are likely to have, an impact on the activities you have listed. What information do you need about these factors in order to assess impact? For example, economic factors may be driving up the cost of providing a particular service so you will want to know whether these particular economic factors are likely to continue. In this case you would seek economic forecasts from reliable sources. Don't forget, however, that social and economic factors might reduce the need for the particular service! This means you will need to think carefully about the information you might need: it will always be more than you initially thought. Unless you are carrying out this activity as part of your professional work, you may need to prioritise your information needs. It may be useful to discuss the information needs you have identified with colleagues to gain a more complete picture – and to help you to prioritise. Under each of the STEEP factors in Table 17.2 in the columns labelled 1–5 note down what information you will need to assess the likely impact of different external environmental forces on each of the activities you identified in Step 1. You will need to spend about 30 minutes on Step 2.

Step 3. Now you need to seek the information you have identified and interpret it in terms of trends and possible impact on the primary activities you listed. Relatively-accessible sources of information on the external environment include: government statistics (for statistics compiled by the UK government go to http://www.statistics.gov.uk/); newspapers; or the webpages of television channels. In the UK, the BBC or Channel 4 are suitable. You can also try to find other online information by doing a web search but make sure the sources of information you choose are likely to be trustworthy. Another useful source of information may be your colleagues.

It will be for you to decide when you have sufficient information in order to assess trends in external environmental factors and the impact on the primary activities of your organisation now and over the next two years. However, you do not need a lot of detail if you have carried out Steps 1 and 2 with care. Knowing that, for example, restrictions on vehicle emissions in a city centre are likely to be extended to the urban areas in which your organisation operates is sufficient to reveal the trend and the impact on your organisation in terms of the cost of modifying or replacing its fleet of delivery vans. Under each of the STEEP factors in Table 17.2 in the columns labelled 1–5 note down the trends you found and, below the trend, note down the likely impact. Be sure to insert the trend and impact under the appropriate STEEP factor and the relevant primary activity. Note that, in the example given, you would list restrictions on vehicle emissions under the primary activity 'logistics' or 'delivery', and you would probably list such restrictions under the 'political' STEEP factor rather than 'natural environment' even though air quality (social, economic) and climate change (natural environment) may have prompted more restrictive political policies. You may also find trends in other external factors that will reduce the impact of an external factor. For example, restrictions of vehicle emissions would be unlikely unless policymakers knew that technical improvements to reduce emissions were likely.

This is likely to be the most time-consuming part of this activity and you should allow up to three hours for it. However, you do not need to do this all in one session. You can check one potential source of information at a time, thus breaking down this step into more manageable chunks.

Step 4. Now think about what you consider to be your organisation's strengths and weaknesses. What is it good at? What is it not so good at? You may find it helpful to discuss these strengths and weaknesses with a colleague. Or you can use the value chain in Figure 13.7 in Reading 4, *Assessing the impact of STEEP factors*. Do not spend too much time on it if you find it too complex to use. Just think through the primary activities in Figure 13.6 which is simpler. Then enter the strengths and weaknesses you have identified in the two corresponding quadrants of the SWOT matrix in Table 17.2.

Step 5. Now, identify what you consider to be key threats and opportunities for your organisation in the next two years. You can do this from the results of Steps 2 and 3, the environmental scanning exercise. Enter these in the remaining quadrants of the SWOT matrix in Table 17.2.

Step 6. Next, think about which of the strengths you have identified would help your organisation to exploit the opportunities and counter the threats you have identified, and which weaknesses might stop your organisation from exploiting opportunities or make it more vulnerable to threats. Note down these in the appropriate row in Table 17.2.

Step 7. Finally, consider anything you, or your part of the organisation, can do over the next two years to help the organisation to adapt to changes in the external environment. Make a brief note on your thoughts and add it in the final row of Table 17.2.

Table 17.2 Environmental scanning and SWOT analysis

Step 1	**Primary activities of the organisation**	**1**	**2**	**3**	**4**	**5**
Steps 2 and 3	**Social environment**	Information needed: Trends: Impacts on organisation:	Information needed: Trends: Impacts on organisation:	Information needed: Trends: Impacts on organisation:	Information needed: Trends: Impacts on organisation:	Information needed: Trends: Impacts on organisation:
	Technological environment	Information needed: Trends: Impacts on organisation:	Information needed: Trends: Impacts on organisation:	Information needed: Trends: Impacts on organisation:	Information needed: Trends: Impacts on organisation:	Information needed: Trends: Impacts on organisation:
	Economic environment	Information needed: Trends: Impacts on organisation:	Information needed: Trends: Impacts on organisation:	Information needed: Trends: Impacts on organisation:	Information needed: Trends: Impacts on organisation:	Information needed: Trends: Impacts on organisation:
	Natural environment	Information needed: Trends: Impacts on organisation:	Information needed: Trends: Impacts on organisation:	Information needed: Trends: Impacts on organisation:	Information needed: Trends: Impacts on organisation:	Information needed: Trends: Impacts on organisation:

Table 17.2 continued

	Political environment	Information needed: Trends: Impacts on organisation:	Information needed: Trends: Impacts on organisation:	Information needed: Trends: Impacts on organisation:	Information needed: Trends: Impacts on organisation:	Information needed: Trends: Impacts on organisation:

Step 4 SWOT analysis

Strengths	Weaknesses
Opportunities	Threats

Step 5 How strengths and weaknesses can help or hinder dealing with opportunities and threats

Step 6 Potential changes to help adaptation to trends in the external environment

This activity is complex and was possibly challenging to carry out, particularly as you may have had to make do with less than complete or ideal information. But perhaps you also found the activity satisfying. Environmental scanning – and looking at how we can meet the opportunities and threats that factors in the external environment can bring – can help us to feel aware and prepared. All of this week's activities are relevant to managing change, the topic of the final two weeks of reading and activities, and of the end-of-module assessment (EMA).

Activity 2 output

- *A completed version of Table 17.2.*

Activity 3

Allow 30 minutes for this activity.

This activity focusses on sustainability and climate change. It is designed to encourage you to think in more depth about the way in which you might respond to impact from the natural environment and to share these ideas with other students in the Week 17 activity forum. To prepare for the activity, you may want to refer again to the paragraphs on the natural environment in Reading 3, Figure 13.8, the 'inside-out' version of the value chain in Reading 4, and the sections on sustainability and climate change in Appendix 1 of the Module Guide.

First, consider how you expect sustainability and climate change issues to affect your organisation (or the part in which you work) over the next 10 years and what you think you might be able to do in order to respond to these issues. Then post a message to the Week 17 activity forum setting out briefly the issues and responses. (A message of about 100 words will be sufficient). Read the messages posted by other students in the forum. What issues have they identified? How do they propose to respond?

Now post another message in which you respond to at least one other student, suggesting how each of you might be able to respond better to the sustainability and climate change issues identified.

There is no output table or template for this activity.

It would be satisfying to think that we make appropriate and effective responses to address issues of sustainability and climate change. You may have identified some responses, or you may have realised that a reconsideration of a number of organisational operations is needed. How constrained did you feel by the culture of the organisation, what competitors are doing, the cost of responding, or other factors? It is often the case that how we want to respond does not match what is possible in an organisation. But what would happen if choice were removed by legislation, or if powerful public opinion threatened to reduce the demand for your products or services (or, in the case of some services, consumers refused to pay for them)? Would that make a difference? It is likely that, as issues take on greater importance, our responses to them will be larger and more urgent.

Activity 3 outputs

- *A contribution to the Week 17 activity forum setting out sustainability and climate change issues and potential responses.*
- *A contribution to the Week 17 activity forum with suggestions for improvements to your own responses and to those of one other student.*

Week 17 activity outputs

1. A completed version of Table 17.1.
2. A completed version of Table 17.2.
3. A contribution to the Week 17 activity forum setting out sustainability and climate change issues and potential responses.
4. A contribution to the Week 17 activity forum with suggestions for improvements to your own responses and to those of one other student.

Learning outcomes

After completing this set of activities and readings you should be able to:

- understand the internal, near and far environments in which an organisation operates
- understand how the boundaries of an organisation are affected by a number of different factors
- identify key stakeholders, their interests and their power, the legitimacy and urgency of the claims and conflicts between stakeholder interests
- consider the ethical implications of stakeholder claims and how the organisation responds to them
- understand the external environment
- understand, seek information about and use STEEP factors
- understand and carry out a SWOT analysis
- appreciate issues of sustainability and climate change, and suggest appropriate and effective responses to them.

Week 18 Managing change (1)

Introduction

When an organisation decides to make wide-reaching changes, invariably managers are involved – sometimes by having to implement the changes or by having to comply with them. At other times, they may need to initiate and implement changes at a more 'local' level in their own part of the organisation or in the work group. Your study of the 'three environments' last week will have alerted you to some of the reasons why change is necessary and how much influence or control you have over these factors. This week we consider the kinds of changes that organisations and managers make.

We also examine different approaches to change and then we introduce tools you will find useful when planning changes you want or need to make. These include a method of assessing the factors that will help or hinder a particular change and the potential impact a change can have on other aspects or parts of an organisation. When you make a change, you will want to make sure that you don't create more problems than you hope to solve!

Week 18 Activities

- Activity 1 Reflect on two recent changes to identify your own feelings about them. (Allow 30 minutes for this activity.)
- Activity 2 Assess the different characteristics of these changes. (Allow 30 minutes for this activity.)
- Activity 3 Assess how feasible the two change situations were using a management tool. (Allow 90 minutes for this activity.)

Readings

All readings are in *Managing and managing people*, Chapter 14 'Managing change'.

- Reading 1 Types of change
- Reading 2 Planned and emergent approaches to change
- Reading 3 Merging the planned and emergent approaches: a case study
- Reading 4 The feasibility of change

Activity 1

Allow 30 minutes for this activity.

This activity focusses on your own experiences of being involved in changes that you did not wholly initiate, plan and implement, although you may have been involved in these processes. The activity is designed to help you think about common reactions to change and, therefore, how people may react to changes that you make from now on.

First, choose two examples of change in your organisation in the recent past. They can be of any sort: for example, a reorganisation, a policy redirection, cutbacks, or the introduction of a new system or procedure. Try to choose one change that you welcomed, at least initially, and another that you opposed or had reservations about. Then answer the questions in Table 18.1 by completing columns two and three. Summarise your thoughts at the end of Table 18.1. As you complete the readings and remaining activities this week you can add to or adapt what you have written: you may change your views!

Table 18.1 Welcome and unwelcome change

Question	Welcome change	Unwelcome change
What was your role in the change? Did you help to initiate and plan the change or was it imposed on you?		
How far were you able to influence the change as it developed?		
Was it clear what the change was?		
Was it clear why it was happening?		
Was it clear what it would involve?		
Did the change create conflict and disagreement, or were there positive responses to it?		
Did the change have the intended result (and how did you know)?		
Did it mean extra work for you?		
Was the change personally stressful and threatening?		
What was lost and what was gained in the process of the change?		
Summary		

This activity may have been quite revealing – you may have uncovered strong feelings and reactions to change that you have not expressed before. This is quite usual. Change can be difficult, threatening and stressful. The more skilfully a change is managed, however, the more people can feel a sense of involvement and see the benefits. Getting buy-in and support for change is an important aspect of managing change.

Activity 1 output

- *A completed version of Table 18.1.*

Reading 1

Reading 1, *Types of change*, in Chapter 14 considers different types of change and characteristics of change, together with factors such as certainty and agreement, risk and disturbance. As you read, think about the changes you selected as a focus for Activity 1. This will help you to carry out Activity 2.

Activity 2

Allow 30 minutes for this activity.

This activity is designed to help you think about types of change and reasons for change, and why some changes may be more difficult to achieve than others. Table 18.2 provides questions to help you. First, assess the types of change that you considered in Activity 1 and some of their characteristics, using the table by Ackerman (1997) in Reading 1. Then consider the certainty and level of agreement surrounding the changes. Use the diagram adapted from Stacey (1996) to do this. Finally, consider the diagram by Pennington (2003) and decide whether the changes were core or peripheral, radical or incremental. Note that these dimensions exist along a continuum, so a change need not involve core processes but may not be completely peripheral either. When you have responded to the questions in Table 18.2, briefly summarise the type and key characteristics of the welcome and unwelcome change. Consider your summary of Activity 1 in relation to your summary of Activity 2. What conclusions can you draw?

Table 18.2 Types and characteristics of the changes

	Welcome change	**Unwelcome change**
Of what type was the change?		
What were the characteristics of the change?		
What was the level of certainty?		
What was the level of agreement?		
Was the change core, peripheral, radical or incremental?		
Summary		
Conclusion after considering the summaries of Activities 1 and 2		

We hope the activity helped you to make sense of the experiences you outlined in Activity 1. For example, you may have realised that risk and uncertainty made a particular change seem threatening, or that lack of agreement coupled with lack of uncertainty made the change complicated or even chaotic. The type of change may have been the ultimate cause of this: radical changes to core activities cause the greatest disturbance. If the particular change had been to remedy a problem, and quickly, this might have increased discomfort – or excitement – about the change. You may have concluded that some of the experiences that you outlined in Activity 1 are now more easily understood. Or you may now think that if you had known more about the particular changes, your experience of them might have been different. Developing an understanding of change is important and it may alter your perspective on changes you have experienced, or will experience in future.

Activity 2 output

- *A completed version of Table 18.2.*

Readings 2, 3 and 4

Reading 2, *Planned and emergent approaches to change*, in Chapter 14 explores two approaches to change. Note that, in management literature, they are considered as approaches taken at an organisational level. It is rather confusing that incremental and emergent change can refer to small, local-level independent changes, while emergent change in which changes are incremental is also a strategy for, or approach to, change. It is important that managers are familiar with both approaches. In terms of changes you will want to make in the course of your work, both approaches are relevant. Each can be scaled-down for use by managers at all levels in an organisation.

Reading 3, *Merging the planned and emergent approaches: a case study*, in Chapter 14 shows how emergent change is often a feature of planned change. It perhaps underlines the point made in Reading 1 about the complexity of organisations: it is impossible to plan every last detail of a change. Every aspect of a change will have an effect and some effects cannot be predicted. They will create the need for more change to either remedy a problem or perhaps offer an opportunity. The Zeta case study illustrates such complexity together with the mix of planned and emergent change.

Reading 4, *The feasibility of change*, in Chapter 14 examines some practical ways in which you can assess whether or not to initiate a change by working out its scope and the prospects for its success. As you read consider the two changes you identified and assessed in Activities 1 and 2, and then use the tools in the reading to assess how feasible the changes were. This will help you to carry out Activity 3.

Activity 3

Allow 90 minutes for this activity.

It will be clear to you by now that change is not feasible if there are too many forces that will inhibit it, and if the strength of these forces cannot be reduced in some way. Thus, working out the feasibility of any proposed change is crucial. Activity 3 focusses on this using force-field analysis. Consider the two changes you used in Activities 1 and 2 and consider the driving and restraining forces that operated in each case, including any long-term pressures. These can come from many different sources and from many different stakeholders. Use force-field analysis to do this and show your analyses in Figures 18.1 and 18.2. Choose the point at which the change process began. If this is difficult to remember, try to recall what was said when you and others first heard about each change. You could also talk to other people who were involved. Depending on their role and involvement, their perceptions may be a little different from your own.

When you have completed these analyses, consider any differences between them. Were the forces for change greater in the welcome change than for the unwelcome one? How were major restraining forces reduced (if you know)? How do both the driving and the restraining forces relate to the type and characteristics of the changes (the subject of Activity 2)? Then complete Table 18.3 in about 200 words. Include your thoughts on the way in which the changes were presented, implemented and managed and those involved in the change process – aspects we consider in more detail next week.

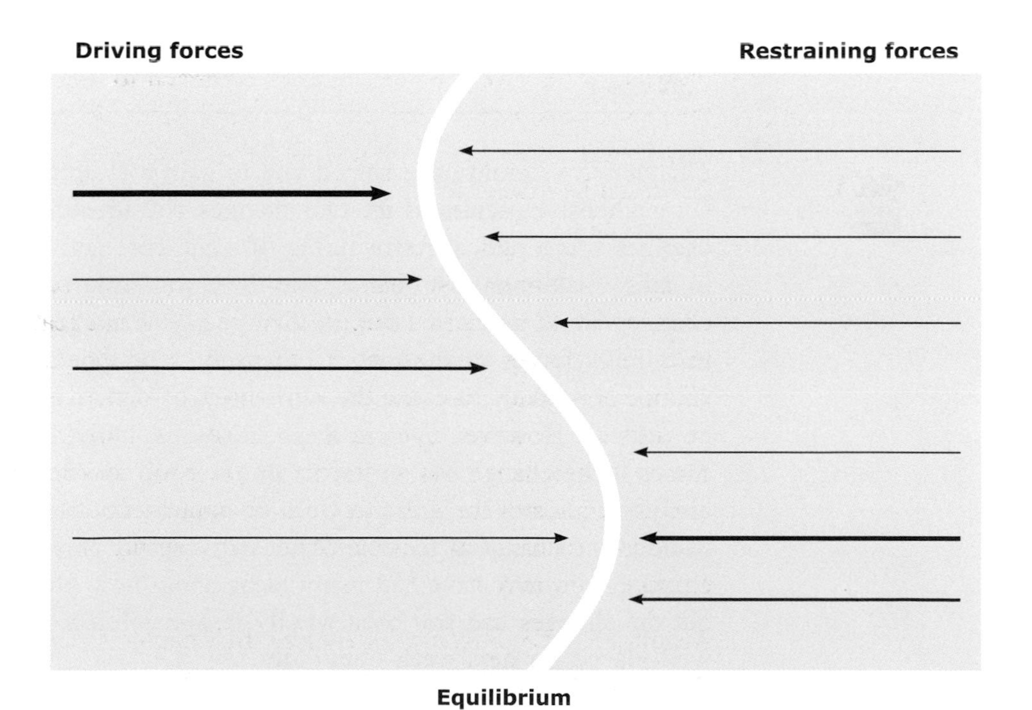

Figure 18.1 Force-field analysis for change 1

(Source: based on Lewin, 1951)

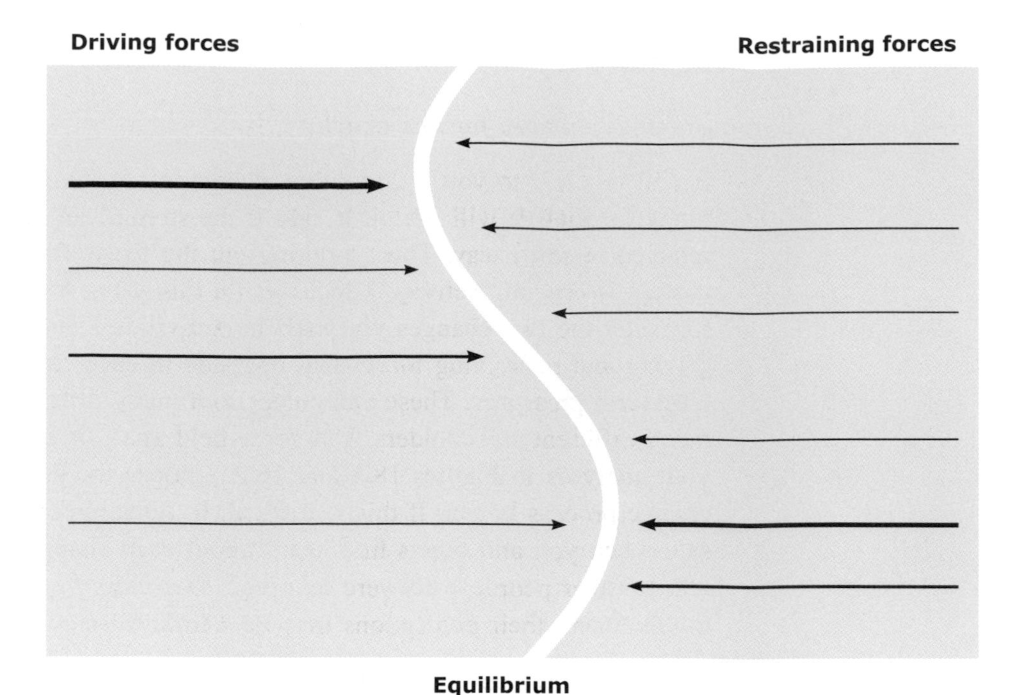

Figure 18.2 Force-field analysis for change 2

(Source: based on Lewin, 1951)

In the writable versions of the force-field diagrams, use the drawing tools in Word to add or delete arrows, to change their thickness, and to label them.

Table 18.3 Force-field analyses: differences and interpretation

Change 1
Change 2

This activity should have helped you to gain a clearer and more comprehensive picture of the two changes you identified. Perhaps one of the changes was a radical restructuring of some core activities which was bound to cause maximum disturbance, and there was little agreement over how the change should be carried out. In this case, you might expect to find that restraining forces were strong. Conversely, a peripheral and incremental change is unlikely to cause the same level of disturbance and is less likely to be resisted. However, even in these situations, individuals may be restraining forces if the change has an impact on their job and status. A force-field analysis indicates the areas to work on to achieve change after you have decided the change is feasible. After carrying out this activity and Activities 1 and 2, you may have had many ideas about how you would have carried out the changes had you been wholly responsible for them. If so, you are well-placed for next week's activities.

Activity 3 outputs

- *A completed version of Figure 18.1.*
- *A completed version of Figure 18.2.*
- *A completed version of Table 18.3.*

Week 18 activity outputs

1 A completed version of Table 18.1.
2 A completed version of Table 18.2.
3 A completed version of Figure 18.1.
4 A completed version of Figure 18.2.
5 A completed version of Table 18.3.

Learning outcomes

After completing this set of activities and readings you should be able to:

- understand and identify types and characteristics of change
- understand the two most common approaches to change management
- assess the feasibility and scope of change
- conduct a force-field analysis.

Week 19 Managing change (2)

Introduction

Is there a change you need to make at work? Perhaps it's one you've been delaying because you fear opposition or because you are not quite sure how best to approach it. Planning and implementing a change can be a daunting task. The challenge for many managers is knowing where to start and how to break the change process down into manageable steps. This week's readings provide practical help, while the activities provide you with an opportunity to identify a change you want to make – a chance to remedy a problem or make a much-needed improvement – and plan how to implement it. As you will see, making successful and effective changes depends to a large extent on matching your approach to change to the context and circumstances and then managing the process with care.

Week 19 Activities

- Activity 1 Outline a proposed change and assess its feasibility and scope. (Allow 90 minutes for this activity.)
- Activity 2 Choose the strategy you intend to adopt for this change. (Allow 1 hour for this activity.)
- Activity 3 Plan for the change using the eight-step model. (Allow 2 hours for this activity.)
- Activity 4 Plan for the evaluation of the change. (Allow 1 hour for this activity.)
- Activity 5 Write a report on the proposed change. (Allow 90 minutes for this activity.)

Readings

All readings are in Managing and managing people, Chapter 14 'Managing change' and Chapter 4 'Planning and control: making things happen'.

- Reading 1 Five operational strategies for change (Chapter 14).
- Reading 2 The eight-step process of change (Chapter 14).
- Reading 3 Dealing with opposition (Chapter 14).
- Reading 4 Evaluation: how well are we doing? (Chapter 4).
- Reading 5 What is being evaluated and how? (Chapter 4).
- Reading 6 Designing a formal evaluation (Chapter 4).
- Reading 7 Some evaluation issues (Chapter 4)

Activity 1

Allow 90 minutes for this activity.

This activity asks you to identify and to justify a change you would like to make in the organisation you work for, or your part of it, and assess the feasibility and scope of the change.

The change should be one that you have the authority to make and that you will have control over. Your feasibility study should help you to determine this. The change may relate to any aspect of the activities you manage. It can be a change to processes, the structure of the work group, systems, or any aspect of managing the people you are responsible for (or work with).

If necessary, you can base the activity on an organisation, or part of one, that you belong to, such as a club, association or voluntary organisation. In such a case, you may not have formal authority or control and you will need to take account of this in Activity 1 and the activities that follow. Here are some steps to guide you through Activity 1. Use Table 19.1 for your output for each step, except where otherwise specified.

Step 1. Identify and describe a current situation that is unsatisfactory in some way or that can be improved, and which requires a change to be made. Sometimes it helps to discuss the current situation with colleagues to identify what the nature of the problem is and consider different solutions.

Step 2. Analyse the situation. Why is the situation unsatisfactory? Analysing what is wrong will help you to decide what needs to be changed or improved.

Step 3. When you have described the current situation, describe the desired situation. This will help you to develop objectives for the change you want to make.

Step 4. Consider the scope of the change, using Leavitt's diamond (in Chapter 14). If you find that the scope of the change is too great, consider whether a smaller change would bring about many of the same benefits or if you would need to involve others in authority. The greater the scope of a change, the more difficult it will be to achieve it. Outline the scope of the change in the fourth row of Table 19.1.

Step 5. Conduct a force-field analysis for your change to assess what the driving and restraining forces for the change might be. Use Figure 19.1 for this. In the writable version use the drawing tools in Word to add or delete arrows, to change the thickness of them, and to label them.

Step 6. Consider and note which of the restraining forces you might need to influence to reduce potential opposition to the change. If your force-field analysis shows that resistance might be too great and potential opponents are difficult to influence, consider adjusting the change or selecting another one. Add details of the restraining forces to the fifth row of Table 19.1.

These six steps will have helped you to identify and analyse a problem that can be resolved by making a change, the change that is needed and the feasibility of the change – the scope and the likelihood of success. Your notes and outputs can be used in the final activity this week which is problem-based.

Table 19.1 A desired change and feasibility

Current situation
Analysis of current situation
Desired situation
Scope of the change
Restraining forces

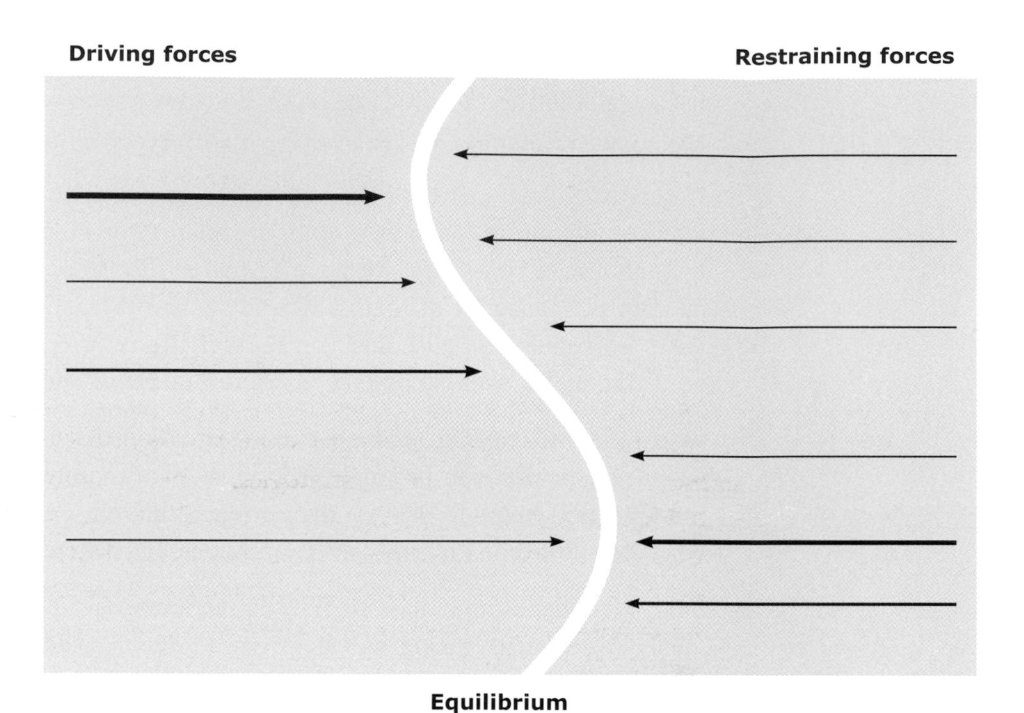

Figure 19.1 Force-field analysis

(Source: based on Lewin, 1951)

Clarifying where you are (present state) and where you want to be (desired or future state), why, and how change can be brought about are the preliminary activities in planning a successful change process. It is likely that you had to go through some of the steps more than once to arrive at a change you can justify. It is important to select a change that does not have too many factors that are outside your control and influence, and is one that is unlikely to meet with insurmountable opposition. You might even have doubted that the desirable change was worth making. This is quite usual, and it is one important reason why managers delay making necessary changes.

Activity 1 outputs

- *A completed version of Table 19.1.*
- *A completed version of Figure 19.1.*

Reading 1

Reading 1, *Five operational strategies for change*, in Chapter 14 sets out various strategies you can use to make the change you identified in Activity 1. As you read, think about which of these strategies you would be most likely to adopt; for example, you may be naturally inclined towards directive strategies. Consider why this might be. Do you generally prefer one particular strategy? Is it a strategy that fits the culture of your organisation? Is it a strategy that fits the circumstances and context of the change you want to make? You will need to balance these considerations when you decide what strategy might be most appropriate for your proposed change.

Activity 2

Allow 1 hour for this activity.

This activity asks you to decide on a strategy or strategies you would ideally adopt when you conduct the change you identified in Activity 1, and to justify the strategy or strategies. When considering the best strategy to adopt, consider the table in Reading 1, *Five operational strategies for change*, which outlines the advantages and disadvantages of each. You should also consider the change strategy continuum in the same reading. Take account of the culture or the organisation you work for, or your part of it, the nature of the change you want to make, and your preferred strategy as well. Your preferred strategy will probably influence how well you are able to adopt other strategies: it may be hard to adopt a participative strategy if you would normally use a directive strategy and vice versa. However, consider how you might overcome the difficulties of using a non-preferred strategy. When you have chosen a strategy or strategies, indicate your choice and give reasons for it in about 250 words. Use Table 19.2 for this.

Table 19.2 Choice of operational strategy or strategies

The operational strategy or strategies I intend to adopt
Reasons for my choice

This activity will have both added to your analysis of the problem and taken you through the stage where you are drawing conclusions from the analysis.

Activity 2 output

- *A completed version of Table 19.2.*

Readings 2 and 3

Reading 2, *The eight-step process of change*, in Chapter 14 draws together many of the concepts and approaches to which you have been introduced and sets out how you can manage a change process. As you read, consider how each of these steps might apply to the change project you are exploring. Note the 'change equation'. It would be worthwhile to use it for the change you are planning. Reading 3, Dealing with opposition, in Chapter 14 deals with resistance to change, possible reasons for it and how you can address it. Note that opposition can be constructive, so it is useful to reflect on it. Consider also the potential opposition you identified when you conducted your force-field analysis and the ways in which you might deal with it.

Activity 3

Allow 2 hours for this activity.

In this activity you will develop plans for the change you identified in Activity 1. Use the first six steps of the eight-step process of change to plan the change. (These can take the form of recommendations.) You will need to make sure that each step takes account of the change strategy or strategies you chose in Activity 2 and the reasons for your choice. While you are working through each step, consider the advantages and disadvantages and implications of your recommendations. Use Table 19.3 to note the results of each step.

Step 1. Start by planning how you will establish a sense of urgency for your change. Consider the change equation in Reading 2, *The eight-step process of change*, and use this to ask yourself the following questions:

- Are others dissatisfied with the way things are? If they are not, why not?
- What other information would you need to provide to create this sense of urgency?
- Does everyone have a shared vision of the future or are there different visions? Check this by speaking to others if necessary.
- Has the change been broken down into steps and if so is there an acceptable first step?
- What are the perceived costs to others?

Part of your plan to establish a sense of urgency should include how you intend to deal with any issues raised in response to these questions. If you decide that a sense of urgency is not needed, or might be unhelpful, make a note of why you think this is so.

Step 2. Use the stakeholder analysis tool in Chapter 13 to identify who you will need to influence. Draw up a plan of how you will go about this. Consider who will join a guiding coalition.

Step 3. Create the vision for your change. To do this, start by considering the desired situation and what makes it so attractive. Then try to clarify this and simplify it to a single statement. Test your vision in discussion with some of those who will be involved in the change (you may have already done this as part of Step 1). They may feel your vision is unclear. Seek the views of the critics as well: these can often be more useful.

Step 4. Communicate the vision. Consider who you will need to communicate with and draw up a communication plan using many different communication channels. Don't forget to include general daily conversations and impromptu opportunities. You cannot plan these discussions specifically, but they can be part of your plan.

Step 5. Draw up a commitment plan using the process set out in Reading 2. First, list the people who are likely to be affected by the change and assess their level of commitment. Then draw up a sub-plan for building alliances.

Step 6. Plan for and create short-term wins. Consider what short-term gains can be achieved as a result of the change, for example, particular quality or performance improvements. Set out the goals and how you will recognise and reward the achievement of them by the staff involved. This will help to prepare you for the next activity in which you take a longer-term perspective and plan the evaluation of the effectiveness of the entire change project.

When you have completed all six steps, write down the advantages, disadvantages and implications of your plan. You are now almost ready to write your report in which you identify a situation that requires change, your analysis of it, your conclusion, your recommended solution and your implementation plan.

Table 19.3 Outline of implementation plan

Establish a sense of urgency
Create a powerful guiding coalition
Develop a vision for change
Communicate the vision
Empower others to act on the vision (including dealing with resistance)
Plan for and create short-term wins
Advantages, disadvantages and implications

(Source: based on Kotter, 1995)

By completing Table 19.3, you will have outlined an implementation plan (or recommendations) that will be effective for the change you want to make. Note that it is only an outline: if you want to implement the change you will need to use detailed planning techniques covered in Chapter 4. But there is one last task: an important one that is frequently overlooked. This is deciding how you will evaluate the change.

Activity 3 output

- *A completed version of Table 19.3.*

Readings 4, 5, 6 and 7

The final readings this week, all in Chapter 4, cover evaluation: Reading 4, *Evaluation: how well are we doing?* sets out the differences between monitoring and evaluation. Note how close they can be when work is ongoing: evaluation doesn't have to wait until a project or task is finished. Reading 5, *What is being evaluated and how?* covers different types of evaluation: note here that the type of evaluation you choose will depend on your objectives. Are you evaluating outcomes or processes? Assessing the processes used in a change, or the effectiveness or impact of the outcome, or both, allows you to draw valuable lessons for next time. Reading 6, *Designing a formal evaluation*, introduces you to the stages of evaluation. You may not want to evaluate your change project in such a formal way as the text sets out, but the stages and processes apply even if you collect the evaluation information informally. You will need to plan. Reading 7, *Some evaluation issues*, will be particularly important if the change you want to make involves many stakeholders from funders to service uses who expect to be consulted and who may all want different things from an evaluation. This is often the case in the public or not-for-profit sectors. While you are reading consider how you might evaluate the change you have been planning in this week's activities. It may be helpful to look ahead to the questions in Activity 4 and try to answer these as you read.

Activity 4

Allow 1 hour for this activity.

Your fourth activity this week is to design an evaluation of the effectiveness of your proposed change. To do this, consider the following questions.

- What do you want to evaluate?
- What will you measure? When considering this, you might like to return to your objectives for the change (your justification for it) and decide whether these are sufficiently clear.
- What sources of information will be needed?
- Who should you involve in the evaluation?
- Who should conduct it?
- Over what timescale will the evaluation take place?
- How are you going to disseminate the results of your evaluation and to whom?
- What issues might arise from taking the evaluation approach you choose to adopt?

Using your responses to these questions, draw up an evaluation plan. There is no template for this. Set out your plan in a Word document. It should be about 250 words in length. Working on this evaluation plan is likely to have honed your thinking about the purpose of the change you are planning, how you intend to go about it and whether, when implemented, it will have the effect you hope. Evaluation, of whatever type (strategy, impact, performance or process), requires clear and precise thinking. You will have had to establish markers to allow you to judge success or otherwise. You may well have considered adjusting your outputs from earlier activities. However, you have the opportunity in Activity 5 to bring together the results of all four activities into a report – your last activity before you write your EMA. You might like to look at what is required for the EMA: Part 1 is based on a change management project of your choosing. Thus, the Activity 5 report will be very useful when you work on the final assessment for this module.

Activity 4 output

- *A Word document containing your evaluation plan.*

Activity 5

Allow 90 minutes for this activity.

For this final activity you will draw the results of Activities 1–4 into a report. Use the report format in Table 19.4 for this, adding additional sections as necessary. Your completed report should be about 1,000 words long including any tables containing text, but excluding the cover page, summary, contents page, references, appendices and any diagrams. Use diagrams where these illustrate a point more clearly than a written description or explanation. Take care to include the main difficulties you expect to encounter and how you will deal with them. Include an evaluation plan (you may need to create another report section or subsection for this). The report will be the most complex you have had to write during this module but it will provide a sound basis for your EMA. Refer either to the guidance provided for Week 4, Activity 4 to ensure that you include the appropriate information in each part of the report, or to the guidance on writing your EMA.

Table 19.4 Report on proposed change project

Cover page
Summary
Contents
Introduction
Analysis
Conclusions to the analysis
Recommendations
Advantages, disadvantages and implications
References

Congratulations! You have achieved much this week, and you may have planned a change project well enough to feel confident that you can carry it out successfully. You have also prepared for the EMA. Not only that, you have completed all the readings and weekly module activities. We hope that you have learned much on your journey – and that you have been able to apply at work what you have learned on this module. If so, then during your weeks of study you will have truly become a more effective manager.

Activity 5 output

- *A completed version of Table 19.4.*